COFFEE CUP BIBLE STUDIES

Chai with
Malachi

AMG
PUBLISHERS

SANDRA GLAHN
AND MALIA RODRIGUEZ

Coffee Cup Bible Studies
Chai with Malachi

© 2013 by Sandra L. Glahn

Published by AMG Publishers. All Rights Reserved.

Published in association with MacGregor Literary, Inc.,
PO Box 1316, Manzanita, OR 97130

First Printing, 2013

ISBN 13: 978-089957348-9

Editing and Proofreading: Diane Stortz and Rick Steele
Interior Design: PerfecType, Nashville, Tennessee
Cover Design: Brian Woodlief, Chattanooga, Tennessee

Printed in the United States of America
18 17 16 15 14 13 –WO– 6 5 4 3 2 1

ACKNOWLEDGMENTS

Thank you . . .
- Gary, my love—for partnering with me in every way.
- Malia Rodriguez—for your friendship, and your capable writing and research for the section on the four hundred silent years.
- Dr. Ron (Allen)—for making the prophets of the First Testament come alive.
- Members of Biblical Studies Press (bible.org) and translators of the NET Bible—for your help, apart from which the Coffee Cup Bible Study series would be impossible. Thank you for laboring without compensation so others might grow in the Word. May God richly reward you.
- Dr. Chip MacGregor—for representing me with enthusiasm and good humor, and for your consistent prayers.
- Rick Steele of AMG and Diane Stortz—for your expertise in both the biblical text and in editing content.
- Steve Smith, my intern—for your skillful and cheerful assistance with proofing, editing, research, and sidebar writing.
- And to all who pray that God will use the Word through this series to change lives. May the Lord reward in public what you have done in secret.

INTRODUCTION TO THE COFFEE CUP BIBLE STUDY SERIES

The precepts of the LORD are right, rejoicing the heart;
The commandment of the LORD is pure, enlightening the eyes
(Psalm 19:8, NASB)

Congratulations! You have chosen wisely. By electing to study the Bible, you are choosing to spend time learning that which will rejoice the heart and enlighten the eyes. And while any study in the Bible is time well spent, the Coffee Cup Bible Studies series has some unique elements. So before we get started, let's consider some of them to help you maximize your study time.

About coffee. You don't have to like coffee to use this series for regular Bible study. Tea works too. So does milk. And water. Or no beverage at all. But embrace the metaphor: take a "coffee break"—a bit of downtime away from the routine, designed to refresh you. And you can imbibe alone, but you might enjoy the process even more with a group. More about that coming up.

Life rhythms. Most participants in Bible studies say they find it easier to keep up on weekdays than on the weekends, when their routine changes. For this reason all Coffee Cup Bible Studies contain weekday Bible study questions that require active involvement, while the weekend segments consist of short, passive readings that draw application from the texts you've been studying. Still, the specified days as laid out here serve as mere suggestions. Some people prefer to attend a Bible study one day and follow a four-day-per-week study schedule along with weekend readings. Others prefer to take twice as long to get through the book, cutting each day's selection roughly in half. Adapt the structure of days to fit your own needs.

Community. While you can complete this study individually, consider going through it with a few others. If you don't already belong to a Bible study group, find some friends and start one. Or connect periodically with others who organize short-term online groups. These vehicles give you opportunities to share what you're learning with a wider community and gain from their insights too. One US reader told us she used Skype to have a regular Bible study using the series with a friend in Australia.

Aesthetics. At the author's Web site (www.aspire2.com) in a section designed for the Coffee Cup series, you will find links to art relating to each study. For *Chai with Malachi* you'll discover artists' renderings of the prophet, links to other studies in Malachi, recommended commentaries, and resource material. The more senses you can engage in your interaction with God's truth, the more you'll enjoy it and remember it.

Convenience. Rather than turning in your Bible to find the references, you'll find the entire text for each day included in this Coffee Cup Bible Studies book. While it's important to know your way around the Word, the series is designed this way so you can stash your study book in a purse, diaper bag, briefcase, or backpack, for use on the subway, at a coffee shop, or in a doctor's waiting room.

Why does the Coffee Cup series use the NET Bible translation? Accessible online from anywhere in the world, the NET (New English Translation) Bible is a contemporary translation from the ancient Greek, Hebrew, and Aramaic texts. A team of biblical language scholars volunteered to create it because they shared a vision to make the Bible available worldwide without the high cost of permissions usually required for using copyrighted materials. Any other translation, with the exception of the King James Version, would have made the cost of including the Bible text prohibitive. Only through the generosity of Biblical Studies Press and the NET Bible translators is this convenience possible. For more information on this ministry, go to www. bible.org. (At this site you will also find numerous resources for Bible study and leadership training, including a special section for women in leadership.)

Sensitivity to time-and-culture considerations. When we study the Bible, in addition to observation, interpretation, and application, we must also consider three contexts: the past, the timeless, and the now. Many Bible studies skip the timeless (or theological) context. That is, they start by guiding readers to observe and interpret the words written to the original audience in the past (the exegetical step), but then they apply the words directly to themselves in their contemporary setting (the homiletical step). The result is sometimes misapplication. For example, Paul told slaves to obey their masters, so we might conclude that we need to obey our *employers.* Yet today's bosses don't own their employees, nor do they usually share the same household. Employment is by mutual agreement; slavery is not. So we should probably use the voluntary *submit* rather than obligatory *obey* when referring to an employment context. In the Coffee Cup series, our aim is to be particularly sensitive to the audience to whom the author's mail was addressed, but we also work to take the crucial step of separating what was intended for a limited audience from that which is for all audiences for all time.

Sensitivity to genre. Rather than crafting a series in which each study is laid out exactly like all the others, each Coffee Cup study is structured to best present the genre category we're examining—whether epistle (letter), poetry, Gospel, history, or narrative. The way we study a prophetic work such as the Book of Malachi differs from how we might examine the compact poetry in Song of Songs or an epistle such as Philippians. So while the studies in the Coffee Cup series may have similar elements, each study takes the approach to the text that best fits the genre. Whereas a study in Philippians will include numerous word studies, a prophetic work such as Malachi will focus less on exact terms and more on structural elements, such as God's question-and-answer test that he gave the nation of Israel.

Selections for memorization. A Cuban pastor incarcerated in deplorable conditions for his faith told my friend afterward, "The Word of God was of great comfort. One Methodist pastor took a notebook and a pencil and wrote down all the Scriptures that everyone knew by heart and recorded them for all of us to read the Word of God." In the absence of Bibles, the only access these prisoners had to God's Word was what they'd hidden in their memories—treasure their captors could never take away. Whether we live where Christians endure persecution or materialism's pull tempts us toward apathy, we need God's Word in our hearts to help us stand strong in every situation. So each week you'll find a verse or two to memorize.

A word about Advent. During the four weeks between the beginning of Advent and Christmas, many Christian believers reflect on Jesus' first advent, or coming, and look ahead in preparation for his second coming. Many denominations, especially those in the west, celebrate Advent as a season in the church year that starts on the fourth Sunday before December 25. (The first Sunday in Advent always falls between November 27 and December 3.) In some traditions people use Advent calendars. Some light candles on Advent wreaths. And others decorate Jesse trees, made of small evergreen branches and covered with symbolic ornaments that relate to the prophecies about and/or the family tree of Jesus. (Jesse was David's father, and an ancestor of Jesus). And some do all or a combination of these, in addition to other traditions, to mark the season.

The first Sunday in Advent marks Christian New Year's Day, or the first day of the Christian year, which follows the life of Christ. Each week in Advent has a different theme. Week one is hope, week two is peace, week three is love, and week four is joy. Typically, churches light a candle on the Advent wreath each Sunday in Advent and light the Christ candle in the center of the wreath on Christmas Eve or Christmas Day.

Chai with Malachi is designed for use either individually or with a group at any time of year, but it also includes Advent questions and an article for discussion section in the back for individual or group use during Advent in hopes that readers will draw near to the Lord and "keep the main thing the main thing" at Christmastime.

Are you ready? If so, fasten your seat belt and fly back in time to the ancient Near East, where our journey begins.

INTRODUCTION TO
CHAI WITH MALACHI

"Bah! Humbug!" With these immortal words, stingy Ebenezer Scrooge dismisses the Christmas ideals of restorative justice and charity. But in nighttime apparitions Scrooge must look face to face at the rotten fruit of his miserliness. In *A Christmas Carol*, Charles Dickens tells the tale of a "squeezing, wrenching, grasping, scraping, clutching, covetous old sinner" whom readers love to hate.

Yet what if Scrooge is us every day of the year? We may not mistreat the Bob Cratchits in our lives or contribute to the untimely deaths of crutch-toting Tiny Tims. But do we overspend on stuff and toss only leftovers in the offering plate? When stopped at an intersection where a homeless person stands near our car, do we study our dashboard and pray for a green light—are we content, as I once heard author Shane Claiborne say, "to worship a homeless man on Sunday but ignore the homeless person on Monday"? Do we keep the good news about grace to ourselves, happy to enjoy its benefits but unwilling to risk opening our mouths because we fear people more than we revere God?

From the Book of Malachi readers learn that God's standards for charity and justice far exceed those exemplified by his people after their rescue from a strange land. And through penetrating use of rhetorical questions, the Lord exposes the rationalizations of his people, particularly the stinginess of his priests.

Sadly, not much has changed. His followers still need the reminder to stop squeezing, wrenching, grasping, scraping, and clutching. And the reminder even comes with a promise that if we devote ourselves to the Lord—to doing justice and mercy in his name—we have the hope that the sun of righteousness will arise with healing in its wings.

The back-story. To understand what's happening in the Book of Malachi, a short narrative history of Israel will help us orient ourselves to the text.

Thousands of years before the events in this book take place, Abram, though childless, has a promise from God that he will become a great nation (see Gen. 12). God keeps his promise, but eventually the descendants of Abraham go to Egypt during a great famine, and Joseph feeds them from the pharaoh's storehouses. Joseph's family stays in the Land of the Pharaohs, and over hundreds of years they multiply. Their numbers threaten the Egyptians, who force them to live as slaves.

When they cry out to God, the Lord eventually sends Moses to lead them through the Red Sea and back to their original country—the Promised Land (see Exodus). But when the time comes to enter the Promised Land, the people refuse to trust God and obey him, so they end up wandering for forty years in the wilderness before that generation dies and those remaining finally enter the land God has given them. Moses appoints Joshua as his successor and dies (read the Book of Joshua).

Under Joshua's leadership, Israel marches in and claims their territory. After many successful military campaigns, Israel generally subdues the enemy, and God's people stand clearly in charge. Joshua retires after a decorated military career, and the Lord leads the nation through leaders called judges (this was God's preference; see the Book of Judges) rather than monarchs. But eventually the people insist on having a king, so God lets them have their way (read 1 and 2 Kings and 1 and 2 Chronicles).

At first the kingdom stands united, under the reigns of King Saul, King David, and later King Solomon. But eventually the nation splits into a northern kingdom called Israel and a southern kingdom called Judah, each having its own king. Over the next five hundred years, both faithful and unfaithful kings rule Israel and Judah. As the years pass, the people of both kingdoms become idolatrous and disregard God's law given through Moses. So God sends the enemy to discipline them, as he has warned many times that he would do.

In 722 BC Sennacherib, king of Assyria, captures Israel. And in 605 BC Nebuchadnezzar, king of Babylon, captures Judah and deports its people to Babylon. For decades Israel and Judah suffer, living in exile among a ruthless people. In 538 BC Cyrus, king of Persia, decrees that the Judeans may return to their homeland. So Zerubbabel, their leader, leads the first group back to Judah that same year. Ezra the priest takes the second group back in 458 BC. Nehemiah is appointed governor and brings the third and final group to Judah in 432 BC. (You can find their stories in the Books of Ezra and Nehemiah.)

Most likely it is during the time when Nehemiah lived that God sends his messenger Malachi to prophesy to Judah. From 432–425 BC, Nehemiah is gone from Jerusalem, having returned to Persia. Although the exact date of Malachi's ministry remains unknown, many scholars believe he prophesied during Nehemiah's absence from Jerusalem.

Malachi relays God's judgment against the Judeans. They have disobeyed his law, and their worship is empty. Even though the priests have reestablished worship in the rebuilt temple, the people are apathetic toward God. When it comes to keeping God's commandments, they yawn and say, "Whatever." They marry spouses who don't revere the Lord, withhold even minimum tithes, neglect the Sabbath, tolerate a corrupt priesthood, act indifferently about injustice, and even go after false gods. Apparently they have forgotten what God allowed the enemy to do to their ancestors when he sent them into captivity.

Through Malachi, God probes their spiritual leaders' hearts and reveals their complacency. The prophet proclaims judgment for their corruption and promises that God will speak again through another messenger, one who will prepare the way for the Lord (Mal. 2:17–3:1).

We know something they didn't—that this latter messenger is John the Baptist (Mark 1:3), for whom they will wait four hundred years. And he will prepare the way for the Lord Jesus himself. During the long years between the prophecy and its fulfillment, God remains silent. We refer to this time of silence as the four hundred silent years. While Malachi does not speak God's final word before these four hundred years begin (see Neh. 13), he does prepare the priests and people for the long, quiet centuries. The wait will test and refine God's people as they anticipate the first advent of the Messiah.

Time. Although we don't know the exact year when Malachi prophesied to Judah, his ministry probably took place around 450–400

BC, following the third return from the Babylonian Captivity. More specifically, as mentioned, Malachi probably ministered between 432–425 BC, when Nehemiah was gone from his people, having returned for a season to Persia. Many scholars believe Malachi prophesied during Nehemiah's absence.

The last book of our Old Testament, Malachi forges a connecting link between the Old and New Testaments both by its placement and its content. The book is rich with messianic prophecies, fulfilled about four hundred years after Malachi prophesied.

It's worth noting, though, that Chronicles, rather than Malachi, was and is the last book of Scripture for the Jews. Their *Tanakh* appears in this order: the Pentateuch, the early prophets (in which Judges and Kings classify as prophets), the major prophets. the Book of the Twelve (the minor prophets), the wisdom literature, and the historical books. The Bible books we know as 1 and 2 Chronicles were and are for them one combined book. So the end of the *Tanakh* is what we would refer to as two books—1 and 2 Chronicles. That explains why, when Jesus summarized his people's history of murdering prophets, he said, "From the blood of Abel to the blood of Zechariah, who was killed between the altar and the sanctuary" (Luke 11:51). Abel's death appears in Genesis 4—at the beginning of the Hebrew Bible—and Zechariah's death appears in 2 Chronicles 24—at the end of the Hebrew Bible.

State of mind. Comparing the Book of Nehemiah, set in approximately the same time period, with the Book of Malachi, we find that God's people felt apathetic about their spiritual lives. They yawned when it came to keeping the Lord's commands; their men abandoned God-fearing spouses to pursue younger, unbelieving women; the people lacked reverence in how they viewed money; they tolerated corrupt spiritual leadership; they had a ho-hum attitude about injustice. On top of that, they had the gall to shake their fists at God and accuse him with "You act like you don't love us!"

Author. *Malachi* means "my messenger." The name "Malachi" may be the prophet's actual name, or it could be the designation of an anonymous writer as God's messenger. The Book of Malachi closes out our Old Testament both sadly and joyously—sadly because it exposes the pitiful spiritual condition of God's people, joyously because it reveals the hope of reconciliation between God, Israel, and the entire world.

Repeated name of God. "The LORD who rules over all." This name is repeated twenty-four times in four short chapters.

Main idea. Many centuries before Malachi, Moses laid out the Book of Deuteronomy as a legal contract, listing the blessings and curses God's covenant people would experience if they failed to uphold their agreement with God. Centuries later in the Book of Malachi, we have another legal context, only this time it's set in a court, and the case is God vs. Israel. God, the plaintiff, accuses Israel, the defendant, of breaking a contract. We see the legal case in a three-step pattern that serves as the book's distinctive structure.

- The plaintiff raises the charge against Israel: "You have done this."
- The defendant pleads ignorance: "How have we done this?"
- The plaintiff answers by listing the specific offenses.

Through this three-step strategy we see how God expected his people to give their best. The Lord lays out his case in the form of a test that contains more than twenty questions.

The very name of God used in Malachi, "the LORD who rules over all" (or "LORD Sabaoth") emphasizes what God seeks to communicate—that he is sovereign and he will keep his promises to bless and curse his people. The ultimate desire in doing so for "the LORD who rules over all" is that his name might be known among the nations.

As we draw back the curtain on the first courtroom scene, the formerly exiled people are back in their homeland. They have settled in and rebuilt their homes, their walls, and their temple. They're fat, happy, tolerating corruption, and letting their hearts wander—"squeezing, wrenching, grasping, scraping, and clutching." But not for long. Enter the prophet Malachi.

CONTENTS

Week 1
No More Leftovers   Malachi 1   1

Week 2
What Sacrifice?   Malachi 2   27

Week 3
I Want Your Best Gift   Malachi 3–4   45

Week 4
The Four Hundred Silent Years   69

Leader's Guide   97

WEEK 1 OF 4

No More Leftovers: Malachi 1

Scripture: " 'You also say, "How tiresome it is." You turn up your nose at it,' says the LORD who rules over all, 'and instead bring what is stolen, lame, or sick. You bring these things for an offering! Should I accept this from you?' asks the LORD" (Mal. 1:13).

Imagine you're hosting a big dinner. What if you swung by the cemetery and swiped some dusty plastic flowers for your centerpiece? And instead of serving turkey or ham with pie for dessert, what if you emptied your trash onto the table where the meat platter goes? Do you think your guests would like to dig in? What would your actions say about how you felt about them?

We wouldn't think of treating other humans this way, yet these actions come close to how the children of Israel treated God during the life of Malachi. They offered him wilted stuff. Leftovers. The junk they didn't plan to use for themselves. And then they couldn't understand why he got upset.

In doing so they followed in a long tradition. In fact, the problem of God getting less than he deserves has been around since the beginning. As early as Genesis 4 we read about a *murder* that happened because someone gave God a halfhearted gift.

Eve gave birth to a son, Cain, and to his little brother, Abel. When the boys grew up, Abel shepherded a flock and Cain worked the ground—the farmer and the cowhand. And the story got sticky fast: "It happened in the course of time that Cain brought an offering to the LORD from the fruit of the ground. But Abel brought of the firstlings of his sheep and of their fat" (vv. 3–4, author's translation).

What Abel brought was "of the firstlings." Those were the first-born animals. Abel also brought of the fat portions. Both the firstborn and the fat portions were considered the best.

But Cain "brought an offering to the Lord from the fruit of the ground." It wasn't wrong to bring grain or produce—the text calls what both brothers brought an offering, and later God gave instructions about how to give him grain offerings. The problem was not the kind of gift but the *quality*. Where were Cain's firstfruits? Where was his best? Apparently he just threw together some stuff he'd grown. It reminds me of the time a friend brought week-old donuts to our Bible study as a joke, except Cain was serious.

Imagine farmers bringing windfall pears or average cuts of rhubarb to state fair judges. No way they'd do that! Only the most mammoth squash will do. The quality of what farmers would bring to a competition is the quality God expected from Cain. But Cain tossed together some veggies. Meanwhile his kid brother "cared enough to send the very best." And of course God preferred Abel's offering.

As a result, "Cain was very angry and his face fell." He assumed, as we sometimes do, that God is obligated to accept anything and everything we offer him, even if it's secondhand and ho-hum.

But God is gracious, so he gave Cain a second chance. And did Cain say, "Thanks, God. Let me run to get the better kumquats"? No. After luring his kid brother to a field where no one could hear his cries, Cain murdered Abel in cold blood.

When the Lord showed up after the murder, he did the same thing with Cain that he'd done when Cain's father sinned—he asked a question. "Where is Abel, your brother?" But Adam's son was shameless. He answered, "I dunno," followed by a smart-alecky "Keeper of my brother, am I?" His tone suggested God was unreasonable even to ask.

"What have you done?" God demanded. "The voice of your brother's blood is crying out to me from the ground." As a consequence, he pronounced a curse: the ground would no longer yield produce for Cain. God also said Cain would become a wanderer.

What? God didn't *kill* him?

And Cain's response? "My punishment is greater than I can bear!" Clueless.

The story ends with Cain departing from the presence of Yahweh and settling in Nod ("wandering"), east of Eden. East. That's the direction his parents went when driven from the orchard. So Cain went to the land of wandering, away from the presence of God.

And the Land of Nod is where we would still live had it not been for Jesus Christ. He made it possible, through the reconciliation bought by the most costly, pleasing sacrifice of all time, for us to "go west," back to fellowship with the Father, no matter what we've done.

Humans have a long history of bringing God our leftovers. Millennia after Cain the people in Malachi's day were still trying to get away with ho-hum sacrifices. And have you ever noticed we do it too—ironically, sometimes even more so at Christmastime, the very season set apart for honoring God for giving the greatest gift of all.

Most of us no longer live in worlds where sheep, cattle, and grain represent our income. We trade in money, time, and energy. But no matter what kind of world we inhabit, we serve a God who is worthy of our best. Do we toss out our spare change or give from the first of our income? Do we care for the poor all year or only by donating cans of unused beets during the holidays? Do we give God our sleepiest hours or our most productive energy? Do we faithfully worship every week but ignore suffering humans Monday through Saturday? The New Testament tells us that God wants more than compartments of our lives. He wants *us*—our whole beings—as *living* sacrifices (Romans 12:1–2).

What we give tells a lot about our regard for the recipient. Are you offering all you have to God? Are you giving the Lord your best?

1. What are some signs that indicate love has faded in a relationship?

_____

_____

_____

_____

2. Pray and ask God to give you understanding and insight. Then read the Book of Malachi (included below, from the NET Bible) in one sitting. As you read, underline references to God as the one who rules over all.

Malachi 1

1:1 What follows is divine revelation. The word of the Lord came to Israel through Malachi:

1:2 "I have shown love to you," says the Lord, but you say, "How have you shown love to us?"

"Esau was Jacob's brother," the Lord explains, "yet I chose Jacob **1:3** and rejected Esau. I turned Esau's mountains into a deserted wasteland and gave his territory to the wild jackals." **1:4** Edom says, "Though we are devastated, we will once again build the ruined places."

So the Lord who rules over all responds, "They indeed may build, but I will overthrow. They will be known as the land of evil, the people with whom the Lord is permanently displeased. **1:5** Your eyes will see it, and then you will say, 'May the Lord be magnified even beyond the border of Israel!' "

1:6 "A son naturally honors his father and a slave respects his master. If I am your father, where is my honor? If I am your master, where is my respect? The Lord who rules over all asks you this, you priests who make light of my name!

But you reply, 'How have we made light of your name?'

1:7 "You are offering improper sacrifices on my altar, yet you ask, 'How have we offended you?' By treating the table of the Lord as if it is of no importance! **1:8** For when you offer blind animals as a sacrifice, is that not wrong? And when you offer the lame and sick, is that not wrong as well? Indeed, try offering them to your governor! Will he be pleased with you or show you favor?' asks the Lord who rules over all. **1:9** But now plead for God's favor that he might be gracious to us. 'With this kind of offering in your hands, how can he be pleased with you?' asks the Lord who rules over all.

1:10 "I wish that one of you would close the temple doors, so that you no longer would light useless fires on my altar. I am not pleased with you," says the Lord who rules over all, "and I will no longer accept an offering from you. **1:11** For from the east to the west my name will be great among the nations. Incense and pure offerings will be offered in my name everywhere, for my name will be great among the nations,' says the Lord who rules over all.

1:12 "But you are profaning it by saying that the table of the Lord is common and its offerings despicable. **1:13** You also say, 'How tiresome it is.' You turn up your nose at it," says the Lord who rules over all, "and instead bring what is stolen, lame, or sick. You bring these things for an offering! Should I accept this from you?" asks the Lord. **1:14** "There will be harsh condemnation for the hypocrite who has a valuable male animal in his flock but vows and sacrifices something inferior to the Lord. For I am a great king," says the Lord who rules over all, "and my name is awesome among the nations."

Malachi 2

2:1 "Now, you priests, this commandment is for you. **2:2** If you do not listen and take seriously the need to honor my name," says the Lord who rules over all, "I will send judgment on you and turn your blessings into curses—indeed, I have already done so because you are not taking it to heart. **2:3** I am about to discipline your children and will spread offal on your faces, the very offal produced at your festivals, and you will be carried away along with it. **2:4** Then you will know that I sent this commandment to you so that my covenant may continue to be with Levi," says the Lord who rules over all.

2:5 "My covenant with him was designed to bring life and peace. I gave its statutes to him to fill him with awe, and he indeed revered me and stood in awe before me. **2:6** He taught what was true; sinful words were not found on his lips. He walked with me in peace and integrity, and he turned many people away from sin. **2:7** For the lips of a priest should preserve knowledge of sacred things, and people should seek instruction from him because he is the messenger of the Lord who rules over all. **2:8** You, however, have turned from the way. You have caused many to violate the law; you have corrupted the covenant with Levi," says the Lord who rules over all. **2:9** "Therefore, I have caused you to be ignored and belittled before all people to the extent to which you are not following after me and are showing partiality in your instruction."

2:10 Do we not all have one father? Did not one God create us? Why do we betray one another, in this way making light of the covenant of our ancestors? **2:11** Judah has become disloyal, and unspeakable sins have been committed in Israel and Jerusalem. For Judah has profaned the holy things that the Lord loves and has turned to a foreign god! **2:12** May the Lord cut off from the community of Jacob every last person who does this, as well as the person who presents improper offerings to the Lord who rules over all!

2:13 You also do this: You cover the altar of the Lord with tears as you weep and groan, because he no longer pays any attention to the offering nor accepts it favorably from you. **2:14** Yet you ask, "Why?"

The Lord is testifying against you on behalf of the wife you married when you were young, to whom you have become unfaithful even though she is your companion and wife by law. **2:15** No one who has even a small portion of the Spirit in him does this. What did our ancestor do when seeking a child from God? Be attentive, then, to your own spirit, for one should not be disloyal to the wife he took in his youth. **2:16** "I hate divorce," says the Lord God of Israel, "and the one who is guilty of violence," says the Lord who rules over all. "Pay attention to your conscience, and do not be unfaithful."

2:17 You have wearied the Lord with your words. But you say, "How have we wearied him?" Because you say, "Everyone who does evil is good in the Lord's opinion, and he delights in them," or "Where is the God of justice?"

Malachi 3

3:1 "I am about to send my messenger, who will clear the way before me. Indeed, the Lord you are seeking will suddenly come to his temple, and the messenger of the covenant, whom you long for, is certainly coming," says the Lord who rules over all.

3:2 Who can endure the day of his coming? Who can keep standing when he appears? For he will be like a refiner's fire, like a launderer's soap. **3:3** He will act like a refiner and purifier of silver and will cleanse the Levites and refine them like gold and silver. Then they will offer the Lord a proper offering. **3:4** The offerings of Judah and Jerusalem will be pleasing to the Lord as in former times and years past.

3:5 "I will come to you in judgment. I will be quick to testify against those who practice divination, those who commit adultery, those who break promises, and those who exploit workers, widows, and orphans, who refuse to help the immigrant and in this way show they do not fear me," says the Lord who rules over all.

3:6 "Since, I, the Lord, do not go back on my promises, you, sons of Jacob, have not perished. **3:7** From the days of your ancestors you have ignored my commandments and have not kept them! Return to me, and I will return to you," says the Lord who rules over all.

"But you say, 'How should we return?'

3:8 "Can a person rob God? You indeed are robbing me, but you say, 'How are we robbing you?' In tithes and contributions! **3:9** You are bound for judgment because you are robbing me—this whole nation is guilty.

3:10 "Bring the entire tithe into the storehouse so that there may be food in my temple. Test me in this matter," says the Lord who rules over all, "to see if I will not open for you the windows of heaven and pour out for you a blessing until there is no room for it all. **3:11** Then I will stop the plague from ruining your crops, and the vine will not lose its fruit before harvest," says the Lord who rules over all. **3:12** "All nations will call you happy, for you indeed will live in a delightful land," says the Lord who rules over all.

3:13 "You have criticized me sharply," says the Lord, "but you ask, 'How have we criticized you?' **3:14** You have said, 'It is useless to serve God. How have we been helped by keeping his requirements and going about like mourners before the Lord who rules over all? **3:15** So now we consider the arrogant to be happy; indeed, those who practice evil are successful. In fact, those who challenge God escape!'"

3:16 Then those who respected the Lord spoke to one another, and the Lord took notice. A scroll was prepared before him in which were recorded the names of those who respected the Lord and honored his name. **3:17** "They will belong to me," says the Lord who rules over all, "in the day when I prepare my own special property. I will spare them as a man spares his son who serves him. **3:18** Then once more you will see that I make a distinction between the righteous and the wicked, between the one who serves God and the one who does not.

Malachi 4

4:1 (3:19) "For indeed the day is coming, burning like a furnace, and all the arrogant evildoers will be chaff. The coming day will burn them up," says the Lord who rules over all. "It will not leave even a root or branch. **4:2** But for you who respect my name, the sun of vindication will rise with healing wings, and you will skip about like calves released from the stall. **4:3** You will trample on the wicked, for they will be like ashes under the soles of your feet on the day which I am preparing," says the Lord who rules over all.

4:4 "Remember the law of my servant Moses, to whom at Horeb I gave rules and regulations for all Israel to obey.

4:5 "Look, I will send you Elijah the prophet before the great and terrible day of the Lord arrives. **4:6** He will encourage fathers and their children to return to me, so that I will not come and strike the earth with judgment."

• *The Lord who rules over all* (1:4). Here God refers to himself as "Lord Sabaoth." The final *h* is silent—Tsuh-vah-*oht*. In Martin Luther's great hymn "A Mighty Fortress," we sing, "Lord Sabaoth his name/From age to age the same,/And he must win the battle." "Lord Sabaoth" or "the Lord of hosts" is how scholars sometimes translate this name for God found throughout Malachi. The word *hosts* refers to the angelic army, as in "hosts of angels." Eugene Peterson in *The Message* renders this name of God as "God-of-the-Angel-Armies." The very name God uses to refer to himself reminds Malachi's listeners, living in a time of great rulers, that he is sovereign over all.

3. What does it mean that God rules over all—geographically, spiritually, materially? List some things in your life included in that "all."

_____

_____

_____

4. What indications do you see that the people to whom Malachi speaks have allowed their relationship with God to deteriorate?

_____

_____

_____

_____

TUESDAY: REMEMBRANCE OF THINGS PAST

In the Book of Malachi, we find a concern for the reputation of "the LORD who rules over all" among the nations. The people's shoddy worship and secondhand gifts have had a negative effect on his reputation. So for his myopic people, he lays out the greater vision. Note the areas in bold type below.

1:5 Your eyes will see it, and then you will say, 'May the LORD be **magnified even beyond the border** of Israel!'

1:11 For from the **east to the west my name will be great among the nations.** Incense and pure offerings will be offered in **my name everywhere**, for **my name will be great among the nations,**" says the LORD who rules over all.

. . . .

3:12 "All nations will call you happy, for you indeed will live in a delightful land," says the LORD who rules over all.

1. What does God's concern for his reputation among the nations suggest about his desire to use the chosen nation of Israel?

_____

_____

_____

2. Pray for insight and read Malachi 1:1–5. Look for the first of God's exams in the form of an accusation, the people's defense, and God's response.

> **1:1** What follows is divine revelation. The word of the Lord came to Israel through Malachi:
>
> **1:2** "I have shown love to you," says the Lord, but you say, "How have you shown love to us?"
>
> "Esau was Jacob's brother," the Lord explains, "yet I chose Jacob **1:3** and rejected Esau. I turned Esau's mountains into a deserted wasteland and gave his territory to the wild jackals."
>
> **1:4** Edom says, "Though we are devastated, we will once again build the ruined places." So the Lord who rules over all responds, "They indeed may build, but I will overthrow. They will be known as the land of evil, the people with whom the Lord is permanently displeased. **1:5** Your eyes will see it, and then you will say, 'May the Lord be magnified even beyond the border of Israel!' "

3. To whom and through whom was the Book of Malachi written (1:1)?

_____

_____

- *Esau* (1:2). The Israelites were and are descendants of Isaac. As you may recall, Isaac had two sons, Jacob and Esau. Esau's descendants came to be called Edomites. *Edom* means "red," which makes sense because Esau was a hairy, red-headed guy. Perhaps his nickname was even *Red.* (Read Genesis 27 to learn more about these brothers.) The Edomites were relatives who went on to be Israel's enemies, as recorded in Ehud's story in the Book of Judges. In the conversation between God and Israel recorded in Malachi 1:2–3, we read, "'Esau was Jacob's brother,' the LORD explains, 'yet I chose Jacob and rejected Esau.'" More literally, Malachi quotes God using a Hebrew idiom ("Jacob I have loved; Esau I have hated").

The contrast between love and hate is perhaps better understood in English as "loved" and "loved less" or "chosen" and "not chosen." Think of a puppy selected (loved) from a pet store and by default the others are not chosen (not loved). The passion for the one "loved more" makes the one "loved less" appear hated in comparison. We see a New Testament example of this kind of thinking where we read that those who do not hate their relatives and love Christ are unworthy (Luke 14:26). The idea is not that God wants us to hate people; it's on the intensity and demonstration of love. The idea here is that God has shown love to Israel by continuing to reject their enemies and foil Edom's plans.

4. What complaint does God have about his people (1:2)?

_____

_____

5. How do the people respond to his first accusation (1:2)?

_____

_____

_____

The Last Shall Be First

It happens all the time in gym class: the least desirable kids get picked last. But God often picks the least likely people first. In Malachi 1:2, God says that he chose Jacob instead of Esau. To us that may not raise an eyebrow, but choosing the younger brother over the older would have made jaws drop in the ancient Near East. Such a choice went against the tradition of primogeniture ("first birth"), the custom that granted the firstborn male the right to inherit the entire estate.

God loves to turn upside down the world's way of doing things. In Scripture we see a number of times when God chose someone other than the expected firstborn to accomplish his mighty deeds. He chose Joseph, Jacob's eleventh son, to become second in command in Egypt and to save his entire family and the nation of Egypt from famine (Gen. 50:20). He chose Judah, the fourth son of Jacob and Leah, to be the one through whose descendants Messiah would come. God chose Moses instead of his older brother, Aaron, to deliver the people of Israel from Egypt (Ex. 3:10–12). And David, Jesse's youngest son, was God's choice as king rather than his impressive older brothers (1 Sam. 16:6–13).

God tends to pick the least expected people first. According to 1 Corinthians 1:26–31, he does this so that we will not boast in our own merits but rather in him. The theme for week one of Advent is hope. How does God's love for choosing the least expected people first give us hope?

6. God chose the Israelites over the Edomites. Locate Edom on a map of Old Testament geography. Ancient Edom became desolate and filled with jackals. The original people were driven out by their enemies, and the area later became known as Idumea (see Mark 3:8). The ones whom God loves doubt that love because they have spent seventy years in captivity. Though God has miraculously returned them to their homeland, they continue to focus on the time of captivity.

7. What are some ways God showed his love to Israel in the past? Feel free to draw on any knowledge you might have of the Old Testament and Israel's wilderness wanderings, or read Psalm 106 as a reminder.

8. What does the Israelites' doubt say about them?

9. What has the Lord done for you in the past?

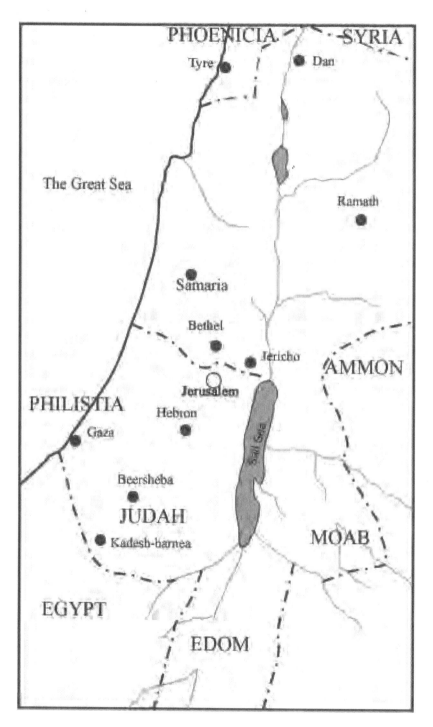

10. List areas in which you, like the Israelites, have struggled to believe or live like you believe God loves you.

_____

_____

_____

_____

11. Based on this passage, how do you think it makes God feel when his people don't believe he loves them? Why is it important to God that his people trust his love and give him our best as an expression of worship and gratitude?

_____

_____

WEDNESDAY: THE GIFT THAT DISAPPOINTS

1. Pray for the Holy Spirit to grant you insight. Then read Malachi 1:6–12.

1:6 "A son naturally honors his father and a slave respects his master. If I am your father, where is my honor? If I am your master, where is my respect?" The Lord who rules over all asks you this, you priests who make light of my name! But you reply, "How have we made light of your name?"

1:7 You are offering improper sacrifices on my altar, yet you ask, "How have we offended you?" By treating the table of the Lord as if it is of no importance! **1:8** For when you offer blind animals as a sacrifice, is that not wrong? And when you offer the lame and sick, is that not wrong as well? Indeed, try offering them to your governor! "Will he be pleased with you or show you favor?" asks the Lord who rules over all. **1:9** But now plead for God's favor that he might be gracious to us. "With this kind of offering in your hands, how can he be pleased with you?" asks the Lord who rules over all.

1:10 "I wish that one of you would close the temple doors, so that you no longer would light useless fires on my altar. I am not pleased with you," says the Lord who rules over all, "and I will no longer accept an offering from you. **1:11** For from the east to the west my name will be great among the nations. Incense and pure offerings will be offered in my name everywhere, for my name will be great among the nations," says the Lord who rules over all. **1:12** "But you are profaning it by saying that the table of the Lord is common and its offerings despicable."

2. If God's first accusation is that his people don't appreciate his love, what is his second complaint against them (1:6–7)?

_____

_____

_____

3. Respecting the Lord's name is one of the Ten Commandments (Ex. 20:7). The Lord's Prayer also includes, "Hallowed be thy name." Most people limit their application of not taking the Lord's name in vain to mean "Don't use God's name when you cuss" or "Don't use God's name as a means of pausing in a sentence or emphatic speech, but only when actually, literally, referring to God." And these would be appropriate applications. But what other actions does God connect with those who "make light of my name" (Mal. 1:6)?

_____

_____

_____

4. What is the people's response (1:7)?

_____

_____

5. Summarize God's explanation of his actions (1:7–12).

_____

_____

_____

_____

6. To better understand what God's people were supposed to do, read the following instructions from Moses' law about the sacrifices God instructed his people to bring.

Deuteronomy 15:21 If [the offerings] have any kind of blemish—lameness, blindness, or anything else—you may not offer them as a sacrifice to the LORD your God.

Leviticus 7:1–20 "This is the law of the guilt offering. It is most holy. **7:2** In the place where they slaughter the burnt offering they must slaughter the guilt offering, and the officiating priest must splash the blood against the altar's sides. **7:3** Then the one making the offering must present all its fat: the fatty tail, the fat covering the entrails, **7:4** the two kidneys and the fat on their sinews, and the protruding lobe on the liver (which he must remove along with the kidneys). **7:5** Then the priest must offer them up in smoke on the altar as a gift to the Lord. It is a guilt offering. **7:6** Any male among the priests may eat it. It must be eaten in a holy place. It is most holy. **7:7** The law is the same for the sin offering and the guilt offering; it belongs to the priest who makes atonement with it.

7:8 "'As for the priest who presents someone's burnt offering, the hide of that burnt offering which he presented belongs to him. **7:9** Every grain offering which is baked in the oven or made in the pan or on the griddle belongs to the priest who presented it. **7:10** Every grain offering, whether mixed with olive oil or dry, belongs to all the sons of Aaron, each one alike.

7:11 "'This is the law of the peace offering sacrifice which he is to present to the Lord. **7:12** If he presents it on account of thanksgiving, along with the thank offering sacrifice he must present unleavened loaves mixed with olive oil, unleavened wafers smeared with olive oil, and well soaked ring-shaped loaves made of choice wheat flour mixed with olive oil. **7:13** He must present this grain offering in addition to ring-shaped loaves of leavened bread which regularly accompany the sacrifice of his thanksgiving peace offering. **7:14** He must present one of each kind of grain offering as a contribution offering to the Lord; it belongs to the priest who splashes the blood of the peace offering. **7:15** The meat of his thanksgiving peace offering must be eaten on the day of his offering; he must not set any of it aside until morning.

7:16 "'If his offering is a votive or freewill sacrifice, it may be eaten on the day he presents his sacrifice, and also the leftovers from it may be eaten on the next day, **7:17** but the leftovers from the meat of the sacrifice must be burned up in the fire on the third day. **7:18** If some of the meat of his peace offering sacrifice is ever eaten on the third day it will not be accepted; it will not be accounted to the one who presented it, since it is spoiled, and the person who eats from it will bear his punishment for iniquity. **7:19** The meat which touches anything ceremonially unclean must not be eaten; it must be burned up in the fire. As for ceremonially clean meat, everyone who is ceremonially clean may eat the meat. **7:20** The person who eats meat from the peace offering sacrifice which belongs to the Lord while his uncleanness persists will be cut off from his people. **7:21** When a person touches anything unclean (whether human uncleanness, or an unclean animal, or an unclean detestable creature) and eats some of the meat of the peace offering sacrifice which belongs to the Lord, that person will be cut off from his people.'"

7. What do the requirements about the quality of offerings suggest about the character of God?

_____

_____

8. How does God feel about the gifts his people are actually bringing (1:9–10)?

_____

_____

_____

9. Why do you think God considers their gifts disrespectful?

10. Interact with this statement: "Any offering or effort that you give God, no matter how small or insignificant, he receives with pleasure." In what way is the statement true, and in what way(s) might it be inaccurate?

THURSDAY: NO FEAR?

1. Pray for insight and read Malachi 1:6–12.

1:6 "A son naturally honors his father and a slave respects his master. If I am your father, where is my honor? If I am your master, where is my respect? The Lord who rules over all asks you this, you priests who make light of my name!

But you reply, "How have we made light of your name?"

1:7 You are offering improper sacrifices on my altar.

Yet you ask, "How have we offended you?"

By treating the table of the Lord as if it is of no importance! **1:8** For when you offer blind animals as a sacrifice, is that not wrong?

And when you offer the lame and sick, is that not wrong as well? Indeed, try offering them to your governor! "Will he be pleased with you or show you favor?" asks the Lord who rules over all. **1:9** But now plead for God's favor that he might be gracious to us. "With this kind of offering in your hands, how can he be pleased with you?" asks the Lord who rules over all.

1:10 "I wish that one of you would close the temple doors, so that you no longer would light useless fires on my altar. I am not pleased with you," says the Lord who rules over all, "and I will no longer accept an offering from you. **1:11** For from the east to the west my name will be great among the nations. Incense and pure offerings will be offered in my name everywhere, for my name will be great among the nations," says the Lord who rules over all. **1:12** "But you are profaning it by saying that the table of the Lord is common and its offerings despicable.

God approaches difficult conversations by starting with questions. When the first humans sinned, he asked, "Where are you?" When Cain killed Abel, God asked Cain, "Where is your brother?" And throughout the Book of Malachi, God confronts Israel. Notice the questions asked throughout the book.

1:6 "A son naturally honors his father and a slave respects his master. If I am your father, where is my honor? If I am your master, where is my respect?

1:8 For when you offer blind animals as a sacrifice, is that not wrong? And when you offer the lame and sick, is that not wrong as well? Indeed, try offering them to your governor! Will he be pleased with you or show you favor?" asks the LORD who rules over all. **1:9** . . . "With this kind of offering in your hands, how can he be pleased with you?" asks the LORD who rules over all.

1:13 You bring these things [what is stolen, lame, sick] for an offering! Should I accept this from you?" asks the Lord.

· ·

2:10 Do we not all have one father? Did not one God create us? Why do we betray one another, in this way making light of the covenant of our ancestors?

· ·

3:2 Who can endure the day of [God's messenger's] coming? Who can keep standing when he appears?

3:8 Can a person rob God?

2. What emphasis do you see in God's questions?

_____

_____

_____

_____

_____

3. What are some ways in which children typically respect parents and slaves respect masters?

_____

_____

_____

_____

_____

4. Twice God expresses his primary concern to his people. What is it (1:11)?

_____

_____

• *Great among the nations* (1:11). The "nations" (*goyim*) are those outside of Israel; presumably they don't know the Lord. In a touch of sad irony, God says the Gentiles will someday worship him. God's people are neglecting proper worship and are acting like unbelievers.

In contrast, the nations will one day offer pure offerings and revere his name.

5. What attitude toward God does Malachi 1 suggest those who fear God should have?

_____

_____

_____

6. The Lord bellows, "My name is feared among the nations" (1:14, NASB). What does it mean to fear God? Sometimes people interpret *fear* to mean "terror." At other times they say it means mere respect. Consider this verse from Psalm 33:

> **33:8** Let all the earth fear the LORD;
> Let all who live in the world stand in awe of him.

Hebrew poetry frequently uses parallelism of thought, two lines that say the same thing using different words. Knowing this, what does this psalm tell us about fearing God?

_____

_____

_____

7. Psalm 96:9 says, "Worship the LORD in the splendor of his holiness; tremble before him, all the earth" (NIV). How might someone misunderstand "the fear of God"? How might knowledge of God's holiness inspire healthy fear?

_____

_____

_____

8. How might the failure of God's people to obey put an obstacle between "the nations" and God?

_____

_____

_____

_____

_____

_____

Background Check

To give you a context for the Book of Malachi, read the Book of Nehemiah.

FRIDAY: UNQUALIFIED TO DO THE JOB

1. Pray for the Spirit to grant you insight. Then read what Malachi has to say to the people about their offerings.

1:6 "A son naturally honors his father and a slave respects his master. If I am your father, where is my honor? If I am your master, where is my respect? The Lord who rules over all asks you this, you priests who make light of my name!

But you reply, "How have we made light of your name?"

1:7 You are offering improper sacrifices on my altar.

Yet you ask, "How have we offended you?"

By treating the table of the Lord as if it is of no importance! **1:8** For when you offer blind animals as a sacrifice, is that not wrong? And when you offer the lame and sick, is that not wrong as well? Indeed, try offering them to your governor! "Will he be pleased with you or show you favor?" asks the Lord who rules over all. **1:9** But now plead for God's favor that he might be gracious to us. "With this kind of offering in your hands, how can he be pleased with you?" asks the Lord who rules over all.

1:10 "I wish that one of you would close the temple doors, so that you no longer would light useless fires on my altar. I am not pleased with you," says the Lord who rules over all, "and I will no longer accept an offering from you. **1:11** For from the east to the west my name will be great among the nations. Incense and pure offerings will be offered in my name everywhere, for my name will be great among the nations," says the Lord who rules over all. **1:12** "But you are profaning it by saying that the table of the Lord is common and its offerings despicable.

2. What seems to be God's vision for what the people should do as they offer worship (vv. 7–9)?

_____

_____

_____

_____

3. Today we don't bring goats or rams to offer as gifts to God. But he calls us to give him our best. How can you give him your best in these areas, especially during times of the year set apart for honoring Christ (e.g., Christmas, Easter, etc.)?

Worship

_____

_____

_____

_____

Time

_____

_____

_____

_____

Thinking (including lyrics)

_____

_____

_____

Money

_____

_____

_____

Relationships

_____

_____

_____

Approach to the Lord's Supper

_____

_____

_____

_____

Rest

_____

_____

_____

Outreach to the nations

_____

_____

_____

Your body

_____

_____

_____

_____

4. Take some time today to pray about each of these areas. Ask the Lord to help you take inventory of your life. Worship LORD Sabaoth as the ruler of all, including every part of your life. Ask the Spirit to help you give your best to a great God worthy of awe. Say thank-you for the gift of Jesus—that while humanity was lost, the Father withheld nothing, not even his very best, his only Son.

SATURDAY: LOUSY GIFTS FOR AWESOME GOD

Scripture: For I am a great king," says the LORD who rules over all, "and my name is awesome among the nations" (Mal. 1:14).

Think about birthdays through the eyes of a child. When you were little, did you like chocolate cake with chocolate frosting? Or, like my mom, did you choose lemon cake? My daughter always wants pumpkin pie. And then there are the noisemakers and hanging decorations, not to mention streamers, matching plates, cups, and party hats. (Sometimes our girl would put one of those on the cat. It never stayed.) Despite all the yumminess and the colors, for most children the best part of celebrating a birthday is opening presents. What's the most memorable gift you ever received?

When the great outdoorsman Teddy Roosevelt was president, an admirer sent him a coyote. Unfortunately, when it arrived, it broke free and terrorized the first family and the White House staff!

The first ten years of my life, I grew up in the Willamette Valley, a fertile plain with a river running by our home. We had plenty of water and good soil. My dad worked a government job, but to help support his wife and five kids, he had a one-acre garden in addition to a pear orchard and a Christmas tree farm. He was good at growing produce. Every year he set aside the largest, most exquisitely formed pears to exhibit at the Oregon State Fair. Sometimes his rhubarb was good enough to enter too. Or a mammoth squash would sprout up and make it all the way to the judges' booth. For his displays Dad chose only the biggest and the best—the choicest fruit. And afterward he lined his walls with award ribbons.

When you're heading to the judges' booth, you take your best stuff. And that's the kind of quality God wants from his people. The finest. The best. The stuff they might brag about. You don't take your leftovers to the Judge.

Malachi had a message from the Lord for the people: You've given third-class gifts to a first-class God! I have loved you but you have robbed me!

What is acceptable to God? If we asked the Spirit to tell us his heart's desire, what would top his wish list? No longer does he want animal fat and firstfruits from the harvest. The apostle Paul tells us in Romans 12:1–2 that God wants us—our lives—as *living* sacrifices. More than anything, the Father wants the love and devotion of each human's whole and undivided heart.

What gifts are you bringing to God? Do you need to upgrade your offering as an expression of homage to the king?

Pray: Lord, have mercy upon me for all the times I've given you so much less than you deserve. I repent. And I worship you, the ruler of all, the worthy one, the ever-gracious God. I offer you my body, my mind, my love, my relationships, my possessions, my time, my talents. All that I have is yours and comes from you. Take and use it for your glory. I know that you love me because of all you have done. Thank you! In the name of Jesus, Amen.

Memorize: "May the LORD be magnified even beyond the border of Israel" (Mal. 1:5).

WEEK 2 OF 4

What Sacrifice?: Malachi 2

SUNDAY: IS MY HUSBAND MY PRIEST?

Scripture: "For the lips of a priest should preserve knowledge of sacred things, and people should seek instruction from him because he is the messenger of the Lord who rules over all" (Mal. 2:7).

One so-called feminist idea that we might think came out of the Enlightenment actually came right out of the Reformation: The doctrine of the priesthood of all believers. This teaching opened new ways for men and women to think of women not as intrinsically inferior to men, but as partners called to lead the world to Christ.

In Peter's first epistle we read, "But you are a chosen race, a *royal priesthood* (italics added), a holy nation, a people of his own, so that you may proclaim the virtues of the one who called you out of darkness into his marvelous light" (2:9). Peter was writing to the whole church, not to men only, when he described all his readers as priests. His phrasing harkens back to God's desire for Israel that they would "be for me a kingdom of priests and a holy nation" (Exo. 19:6). God was speaking to men and women there, too.

Meanwhile, in the apostle Paul's first private correspondence with his protégé, Timothy, he wrote this: "For there is one God and one intermediary between God and humanity, Christ Jesus, himself human." Some translations say "one intermediary between God and man . . ." but the word translated "man" here is *anthropon*, a form of the word from which we get "anthropology"—the study of humans. And in this context Paul had in mind humans, not males only. Humans have direct access to God through Jesus Christ. No human other than Christ serves as an intermediary. We can be priests, leading people to God. But we do not stand between the people and God. And that includes husbands standing between God and their wives.

So how might that look in the home? Let's say, for example, a godly husband thinks that he and his wife should abstain from intimate relations for a time so they can devote themselves to prayer. If he were her priest, he might initiate the conversation and guide her, listening to her input, but then informing her of his benevolent final decision. But if we look at how Paul counseled the Corinthians, we read that such a picture is less than ideal. Why? Because the wife has authority (1 Cor 7:7, root: *exousia*) over her husband's body just as much as he has authority over hers—a radical idea in those days, and a serious challenge to Roman views of masculinity (and perhaps to contemporary ones, too). Paul writes, "Do not deprive each other, except by *mutual agreement* . . ." (italics added). So in our example, which happens to match the one example we have in the New Testament of a couple making a decision related to spiritual things, we see the husband and wife are partners. Equals. Sharing authority in spiritual decision-making. And like friends deciding where to eat dinner, neither needs 51 percent of the vote. Paul assumes a spiritually mature couple can decide mutually what is best. No one takes on the role of priest in the sense of mediating. If the two come to an impasse, the husband does not say, "I am charged with guiding you spiritually, so here is my decision."

Yet sometimes people read that the husband is head of the wife, his body, and they see in such language a picture of an intermediary. Some even describe the husband as *the* priest in the home. I once interviewed Eugene Peterson, best known for *The Message*, and he confided,

> At a pastor's conference I told those in attendance that at noon on Mondays, our Sabbath/hiking day, [my wife] prayed for lunch. In fact I think I said, 'I pray all day Sunday. I'm

tired of it. She can do it on Monday.' There was one woman there who was really irate. She said I should be praying and Jan should not be praying because I'm the priest in the family and she's not the priest. That's silliness. You are brother, sister, man, wife, friends in Christ. You work out the kind of relationship before the Lord that is intimate. And no, I don't think there's any kind of picture you have to fit into, that you have to produce. That's oppressive isn't it? After all, this is freedom in the Lord."

For some of us, it's time to "woman up" and take responsibility for our own spiritual lives. Sometimes a wife will shirk responsibility for her walk with Christ and blame it on her husband's failure to initiate as a spiritual leader. Yes, he is a priest to her, but only in the same way she is a priest to him. Every woman who is "in Christ" is a priest who will stand before God and give account for herself. And that idea is not coming out of feminism. It's right out of the holy Word of God.

MONDAY: KEEPING COVENANT

1. Pray, asking the Spirit for guidance. Then read the section from Malachi that will be our focus this week (2:1–16).

> **2:1** "Now, you priests, this commandment is for you. **2:2** If you do not listen and take seriously the need to honor my name," says the Lord who rules over all, "I will send judgment on you and turn your blessings into curses—indeed, I have already done so because you are not taking it to heart. **2:3** I am about to discipline your children and will spread offal on your faces, the very offal produced at your festivals, and you will be carried away along with it. **2:4** Then you will know that I sent this commandment to you so that my covenant may continue to be with Levi," says the Lord who rules over all.
>
> **2:5** "My covenant with him was designed to bring life and peace. I gave its statutes to him to fill him with awe, and he indeed revered me and stood in awe before me. **2:6** He taught what was true; sinful words were not found on his lips. He walked with me in peace and integrity, and he turned many people away from sin. **2:7** For the lips of a priest should preserve knowledge of sacred things, and people should seek instruction from him because he is the messenger of the Lord who rules over all. **2:8** You, however, have turned from the way. You have caused many to violate the

law; you have corrupted the covenant with Levi," says the Lord who rules over all.

2:9 "Therefore, I have caused you to be ignored and belittled before all people to the extent to which you are not following after me and are showing partiality in your instruction."

2:10 Do we not all have one father? Did not one God create us? Why do we betray one another, in this way making light of the covenant of our ancestors? **2:11** Judah has become disloyal, and unspeakable sins have been committed in Israel and Jerusalem. For Judah has profaned the holy things that the Lord loves and has turned to a foreign god! **2:12** May the Lord cut off from the community of Jacob every last person who does this, as well as the person who presents improper offerings to the Lord who rules over all!

2:13 You also do this: You cover the altar of the Lord with tears as you weep and groan, because he no longer pays any attention to the offering nor accepts it favorably from you. **2:14** Yet you ask, "Why?" The Lord is testifying against you on behalf of the wife you married when you were young, to whom you have become unfaithful even though she is your companion and wife by law. **2:15** No one who has even a small portion of the Spirit in him does this. What did our ancestor do when seeking a child from God? Be attentive, then, to your own spirit, for one should not be disloyal to the wife he took in his youth.

2:16 "I hate divorce," says the Lord God of Israel, "and the one who is guilty of violence," says the Lord who rules over all. "Pay attention to your conscience, and do not be unfaithful."

2. Jot down any observations that stand out to you from this passage. What seems to be the emphasis?

_____

_____

_____

3. To whom does Malachi direct the indictment, beginning in verse 1?

_____

_____

4. Does it appear to you from this passage that the spiritual leaders would incur a stricter judgment? Why or why not?

_____

_____

TUESDAY: POOPY PRIESTS

1. Pray for insight and read Malachi 2:1–7.

> **2:1** "Now, you priests, this commandment is for you. **2:2** If you do not listen and take seriously the need to honor my name," says the Lord who rules over all, "I will send judgment on you and turn your blessings into curses—indeed, I have already done so because you are not taking it to heart. **2:3** I am about to discipline your children and will spread offal on your faces, the very offal produced at your festivals, and you will be carried away along with it. **2:4** Then you will know that I sent this commandment to you so that my covenant may continue to be with Levi," says the Lord who rules over all.
>
> **2:5** "My covenant with him was designed to bring life and peace. I gave its statutes to him to fill him with awe, and he indeed revered me and stood in awe before me. **2:6** He taught what was true; sinful words were not found on his lips. He walked with me in peace and integrity, and he turned many people away from sin. **2:7** For the lips of a priest should preserve knowledge of sacred things, and people should seek instruction from him because he is the messenger of the Lord who rules over all."

2. Of what does God accuse the priests (2:1–2)?

_____

_____

3. What does God say he has done and will do in response to their despicable behavior (vv. 2–3)?

_____

_____

Chai with Malachi   31

- *Offal* (2:3). Offal is refuse. It consists of the parts of the animal prepared for sacrifice that are considered inedible to humans, including the dung inside the animal. God is saying he will use part of the offering itself to express his outrage. God adds a touch of irony. He's using not just *any* offal but the very stuff produced by their shoddy worship.

4. What does God say is the purpose of disciplining the priests (2:4)?

_____

_____

_____

5. What qualities are important for leaders of God's people to have (2:5–7)?

_____

_____

WEDNESDAY: BIBLICAL PRIESTHOOD

1. Pray for insight and read Malachi 2:5–9.

2:5 "My covenant with [Levi] was designed to bring life and peace. I gave its statutes to him to fill him with awe, and he indeed revered me and stood in awe before me. **2:6** He taught what was true; sinful words were not found on his lips. He walked with me in peace and integrity, and he turned many people away from sin. **2:7** For the lips of a priest should preserve knowledge of sacred things, and people should seek instruction from him because he is the messenger of the Lord who rules over all. **2:8** You, however, have turned from the way. You have caused many to violate the law; you have corrupted the covenant with Levi," says the Lord who rules over all.

2:9 "Therefore, I have caused you to be ignored and belittled before all people to the extent to which you are not following after me and are showing partiality in your instruction."

2. Of what does God accuse the priests (v. 9)?

_____

_____

3. What does God say he has done and will do in response to their despicable behavior (v. 9)?

_____

_____

4. Read God's instructions about the Levitical priesthood, as seen in Malachi 2:4, Deuteronomy 33:8–11 and Numbers 3:5–13.

Malachi 2:4 Then you will know that I sent this commandment to you so that my covenant may continue to be with Levi," says the LORD who rules over all.

Deuteronomy 33:8 Of Levi he said:
Your Thummim and Urim belong to your godly one,
whose authority you challenged at Massah,
and with whom you argued at the waters of Meribah.
33:9 He said to his father and mother, "I have not seen him,"
and he did not acknowledge his own brothers
or know his own children,
for they kept your word,
and guarded your covenant.
33:10 They will teach Jacob your ordinances
and Israel your law;
they will offer incense as a pleasant odor,
and a whole offering on your altar.
33:11 Bless, O LORD, his goods,
and be pleased with his efforts;
undercut the legs of any who attack him,
and of those who hate him, so that they cannot stand.

Numbers 3:5 The LORD spoke to Moses: **3:6** "Bring the tribe of Levi near, and present them before Aaron the priest, that they may serve him. **3:7** They are responsible for his needs and the needs of the whole community before the tent of meeting, by attending to the service of the tabernacle. **3:8** And they are responsible for all the furnishings of the tent of meeting, and for the needs of the

Israelites, as they serve in the tabernacle. **3:9** You are to assign the Levites to Aaron and his sons; they will be assigned exclusively to him out of all the Israelites. **3:10** So you are to appoint Aaron and his sons, and they will be responsible for their priesthood; but the unauthorized person who comes near must be put to death."

3:11 Then the Lord spoke to Moses: **3:12** "Look, I myself have taken the Levites from among the Israelites instead of every first-born who opens the womb among the Israelites. So the Levites belong to me, **3:13** because all the firstborn are mine. When I destroyed all the firstborn in the land of Egypt, I set apart for myself all the firstborn in Israel, both man and beast. They belong to me. I am the Lord."

5. Based on what you've read, describe God's covenant with Levi.

_____

_____

_____

_____

6. Consider the big picture about priesthood in the Bible. When we talk about biblical priesthood, we usually think in terms of only male pronouns. Isn't being a priest a guy job? A short history helps us answer that question.

In Genesis we meet the first priest of God, the mysterious king of Salem (later, Jerusalem), whom the author of Hebrews says foreshadows our great high priest, Jesus (Heb. 5:10). Genesis 14:18 tells us, "Melchizedek king of Salem brought out bread and wine. (Now he was the priest of the Most High God.)" The priest was the person to whom people brought their offerings for God.

In the days of Moses, God laid out his vision that the entire nation of Israel might serve as a kingdom of priests. God told Moses to tell the nation of Israel, "If you will diligently listen to me and keep my covenant, then you will be my special possession out of all the nations, for all the earth is mine, and you will be to me a kingdom of priests and a holy nation" (Ex. 19:5–6). Everyone in Israel was included.

Eventually, God chose the tribe of Levi, son of Jacob, to serve as the priestly class. He consecrated the Levites by means of a special rite (Ex. 29:1–30), and the Book of Leviticus records their rituals and responsibilities. The tribe of Levi received no land inheritance when Israel settled the Promised Land because God himself was their inheritance.

In the postexilic days of Malachi, God was displeased with what his priests were doing. In announcing his displeasure, he described what priests should do: "For the lips of a priest should preserve knowledge of sacred things, and people should seek instruction from him [literally, "from his mouth"] because he is the messenger of the LORD who rules over all" (Mal. 2:7).

In the New Testament, the apostle Peter gives the post-resurrection vision for all believers as priests of God: "But you are a chosen race, a royal priesthood, a holy nation, a people of his own, so that you may proclaim the virtues of the one who called you out of darkness into his marvelous light" (1 Pet. 2:9). One of the popular phrases used during the Reformation was "the priesthood of all believers." In our current era everyone who names the name of Christ is a priest. And our task? To proclaim the virtues of the one who called us into his marvelous light (v. 9).

7. In what ways do your lips preserve knowledge of sacred things?

_____

_____

_____

8. Can people seek instruction from you because you are a messenger of the Lord who rules over all? Why or why not?

_____

_____

_____

9. In what ways are you proclaiming the virtues of the one who called you out of darkness into his marvelous light? Who needs to hear about him from you?

_____

_____

_____

_____

_____

Thursday: Profaning the Sacred

1. Pray for insight and read Malachi 2:10–16.

2:10 Do we not all have one father? Did not one God create us? Why do we betray one another, in this way making light of the covenant of our ancestors? **2:11** Judah has become disloyal, and unspeakable sins have been committed in Israel and Jerusalem. For Judah has profaned the holy things that the LORD loves and has turned to a foreign god! **2:12** May the LORD cut off from the community of Jacob every last person who does this, as well as the person who presents improper offerings to the LORD who rules over all!

2:13 You also do this: You cover the altar of the Lord with tears as you weep and groan, because he no longer pays any attention to the offering nor accepts it favorably from you. **2:14** Yet you ask, "Why?" The Lord is testifying against you on behalf of the wife you married when you were young, to whom you have become unfaithful even though she is your companion and wife by law. **2:15** No one who has even a small portion of the Spirit in him does this. What did our ancestor do when seeking a child from God? Be attentive, then, to your own spirit, for one should not be disloyal to the wife he took in his youth.

2:16 "I hate divorce," says the Lord God of Israel, "and the one who is guilty of violence," says the Lord who rules over all. "Pay attention to your conscience, and do not be unfaithful."

2. What does God say his people have done to offend him?

_____

_____

_____

• *Do we not all have one father?* (2:10). Malachi is speaking to the Jews: he mentions the "covenant of our ancestors" and refers to Judah, Israel, and Jerusalem (v. 11). Apparently he is appealing to their common ancestry in Abraham (rather than to Adam, the common ancestor of all humanity). Another possible translation is "Did not God make us [Israelites] one?" That is, did not God unite one people? Either way, God made one nation, and when the men in that nation took foreign wives, their actions went against his purpose. God wanted a covenant people to serve as a conduit of his grace to the world, but if his own people went after false gods, how could they be a witness to the one true God?

3. In what way are the people betraying one another (2:10)?

_____

_____

_____

4. Not only have the men taken younger, foreign wives (modern equivalent: leaving believers to marry unbelievers), but it appears they also have divorced older, faithful, Jewish wives to do so. What does God have to say about this (2:14–15)?

_____

_____

_____

_____

• *The wife* (2:14). God uses three phrases in Malachi 2:14 to describe the deserted wife. First, she is "the wife you married when you were young." Second, she is "your companion," and the word for "companion" has the idea of unity at its root. Finally, she is "your wife by law." Commentators have proposed two possible understandings for what this latter phrase means. The first is that the covenant is marriage itself, that the law binds husband and wife, so the sin here is in breaking that intimate covenant. The second option is that "wife by law" refers to the wife being Jewish and chosen from among the covenant people. Thus, the sin is that the men are breaking the national covenant. Both options are plausible. But while the context seems to support the latter, the earlier statement "she is your companion" seems to emphasize the intimate covenant. The men are breaking both commitments—the marriage commitment and the national commitment to God.

God is clearly upset at their cold-blooded behavior. Their godly wives were once beautiful and young. They had left their families, and in an era with no photography, mail service, phones, or e-mail that allowed them to stay in touch. Once these young wives matured and their bodies showed signs of multiple births, backbreaking hours in the sun, and passing years, their husbands replaced them with heathen hotties. They treated their wives as possessions and commodities. God uses words such as *unfaithful* (v. 14) and *disloyal* (v. 15) to describe such behavior.

• *What did our ancestor do when seeking a child from God?* (2:15). Remember what Abraham did when he was childless? He impregnated Hagar—Sarah's Egyptian maid (a foreigner), presumably much younger than Sarah. In Malachi's day, apparently, Abraham's descendants were pointing to their common ancestor as the precedent-setter, justifying their actions by saying, "Abraham did it!"

When Westerners read the Abraham-and-Hagar story, we tend to see it as an example of what can happen when people take matters into their own hands. But that does not seem to be the way the Bible presents it.

First, taking Hagar was not Abraham's idea—it was Sarah's. That alone makes the situation much different from that of Malachi's day. Second, Abraham didn't divorce Sarah, nor does the text say he married Hagar. Third, he didn't go after Hagar because he wanted to be with a "young thang." He wanted something righteous out of the union—"a child," that is, descendants who worshiped the true God, and more specifically a "godly seed"—the very thing Malachi's readers were risking. Finally, the text in Genesis that describes Hagar indicates that she worshiped Yahweh rather than the gods of her Egyptian homeland. She is the only woman in all of Scripture to whom God gives the promise that he will greatly multiply her offspring, and she names the Lord *El Roi*, or "the God who sees.",

Abraham stayed with his wife, sought to increase his descendants for the right reasons, and partnered with a godly woman. The people in Malachi's day were divorcing their wives, unconcerned about godly descendants, and pairing with pagan women.

5. What two things does God say he hates, and what command does he give (2:16)? The context suggests he is equating the two things—that they are not separate.

> **2:16** "I hate divorce," says the LORD God of Israel, "and the one who is guilty of violence," says the LORD who rules over all. "Pay attention to your conscience, and do not be unfaithful."

_____

_____

_____

6. Summarize in your own words what God says in Malachi 2:16. How can we show a high regard for marriage?

_____

_____

_____

• *Guilty of violence* (2:16). The Hebrew text has a word picture here: to "cover with a garment of violence." To "cover" is an Old Testament image for marriage. When a man covered a woman with his garment, he engaged in an act of covenant love. Recall from the Book of Ruth how Ruth asked Boaz to spread his garment over her. She proposed marriage! In Ezekiel 16:8 we find the same image. In contrast, to "cover with a garment of violence" is to do violence to that covenant relationship, which the divorces in this case are doing.

7. God gives yet another reason why he is unhappy with his people (2:17). The text says, "You have wearied the Lord with your words. But you say, 'How have we wearied him?' Because you say, 'Everyone who does evil is good in the Lord's opinion, and he delights in them,' or 'Where is the God of justice?'" What quality of God's character are they doubting? What affect does this have on God?

_____

_____

_____

_____

8. According to the passage you have read today, the people need to

- value truth and justice,
- marry only believers,
- hold a high view of marriage
- trust in God's ultimate justice, and
- seek first God's glory.

Write a prayer of response that includes two things that, by God's grace and help, you can do this week to demonstrate your belief in these ideals.

_____

_____

_____

_____

_____

1. Pray for insight and read Malachi 2:13–16.

> **2:13** You also do this: You cover the altar of the Lord with tears as you weep and groan, because he no longer pays any attention to the offering nor accepts it favorably from you. **2:14** Yet you ask, "Why?" The Lord is testifying against you on behalf of the wife you married when you were young, to whom you have become unfaithful even though she is your companion and wife by law. **2:15** No one who has even a small portion of the Spirit in him does this. What did our ancestor do when seeking a child from God? Be attentive, then, to your own spirit, for one should not be disloyal to the wife he took in his youth.
>
> **2:16** "I hate divorce," says the Lord God of Israel, "and the one who is guilty of violence," says the Lord who rules over all. "Pay attention to your conscience, and do not be unfaithful."

2. What were the results of the men's treacherous behavior (2:13)?

_____

_____

_____

3. How did their actions affect their relationship with God (2:13–14)?

_____

_____

_____

4. What do you think is meant when the text says, "No one who has even a small portion of the Spirit in him does this" (2:15)?

_____

_____

Chai with Malachi   41

5. What command does God give in response to the men's behavior and why (2:15–16)?

_____

_____

_____

6. In Malachi's day men had more social power than women; they generally took the initiative in marrying and divorcing. But today, especially in the West, women have much more control. Consequently, the sort of behavior that Malachi addresses is less gender specific among God's people today than it was in his time. We see professing Christian men *and* women engaging in relationships of serial monogamy, leaving Christ-following spouses for unbelievers, and showing a lack of concern about their testimonies and those of their families. What is God's response to this sort of attitude and action, which does violence to the marriage covenant (v. 16)?

_____

_____

_____

7. Whether you are single or married, ask God to help you hold marriage in honor, to deal justly with others of the opposite sex, and to value God's reputation.

SATURDAY: MALACHI ON MARRIAGE

Often when we talk about a biblical view of divorce, we quote Malachi: "God hates divorce." And it's true. He does. But does that mean God hates the actions of anyone who issues divorce papers?

Most commentators point out that while Moses allowed for divorce (Deut. 24:1–4), he did not intend his allowance as a green light to divorce. Rather, the law was to give the wife some rights in the event that a husband with a hardened heart sent her away. Yet

God himself said he divorced Israel (Isa. 50:1; Jer. 3, and possibly Hosea). If God hates divorce, did he hate his own actions? To answer this question, we need to consider the *context* of Malachi's statement that God hates divorce.

As we have seen this week, Malachi's statement follows an accusation against husbands who chose to do violence to their covenant marriages by divorcing their wives and entering into idolatrous unions. The reason for their divorces: to pursue selfish lives that cared nothing for God's reputation. Yet after they linked up with pagan women, these same men who claimed to follow God cried out to him because he refused to hear them. In this situation we find the principle that's repeated in 1 Peter 3:7, in which the apostle Peter tells husbands to "show them [wives] honor as fellows heirs of the grace of life. In this way nothing will hinder your prayers." In Malachi, men who break covenant with their wives experience unanswered prayer. Peter raises the bar beyond calling believers to avoid divorce in the New Testament and goes deeper to command honor and respect.

Reconciling God's hatred of divorce with his own actions leaves some questions unresolved. We can, however, make two essential observations:

- God divorced only in the case of repeated, unrepentant adultery. What destroyed the relationship was not the divorce per se. The divorce merely called the marriage covenant what it already was: broken.
- God divorced in response to hardness of heart in hopes that his drastic action would bring ultimate restoration for the offending party.

The fact that God divorced Israel leaves room for the option that divorce may be a last resort in addressing the hardness of a spouse's heart. This would explain why in the New Testament we find Paul telling a believer to allow an unbelieving spouse who desires to leave to do so, to choose peace rather than fighting. He grounds this option in our calling: "For God has called us to peace" (1 Cor. 7:15).

As we have seen, in the case that Malachi is addressing, the Israelite men had wives who were faithful both to their marriage covenants and to the Abrahamic and Mosaic covenants. Abandoning such women, and doing so to pursue younger, ungodly women, God viewed as treacherous and violent.

What is your view of divorce? Does it align with Scripture? Whether or not you are married, what is your view of marriage? Do you see it as our culture (even the Christian subculture) often does, as legitimized pleasure that exists only for romance, affection, and self-fulfillment? Or do you view it as a covenant before God, designed to picture Christ and the church (Eph. 5:22–33), and a picture of oneness? If we view marriage as being like an interconnected head and body rather than as a business partnership or a romantic flame, it is more easy for us to see the destruction of such a relationship as an act of violence—a beheading. God is far more concerned about his glory, about faithfulness, about developing godliness than he is about fulfilling all our desires for passion, romance, fulfillment, and desire.

If married, do you honor your covenant before God? Whether married or free, do you respect that a married person to whom you may be attracted is someone else's spouse by law—the law of the land and the law of God? Do you treat marriage with honor or violence?

Pray: Father, thank you for making man and woman in your image and for making the beautiful unity picture of marriage. Thank you for those who model in their marriages a picture of Christ and the church. Please help me to do to others as I would have them do to me where marriage vows are concerned. Help me to honor marriage and to help others to do so. And help me to be counter-cultural, to reflect your glory, in my attitudes and actions about this covenant you have created. Please strengthen your bride, the church, as she models being united as one with your son. Help us to hold marriage in such high regard that others will look to Christians for how to live in unity. Help our leaders to model such loyal love, and help me to do the same. In Jesus' name, Amen.

Memorize: For the lips of a priest should preserve knowledge of sacred things, and people should seek instruction from him because he is the messenger of the LORD who rules over all (Mal. 2:7).

I Want Your Best Gift: Malachi 3–4

SUNDAY: REFINER'S FIRE

Scripture: Who can endure the day of his coming? Who can keep standing when he appears? For he will be like a refiner's fire, like a launderer's soap (Mal. 3:2).

In describing the coming of the Lord, the prophet Malachi used two similes—"like a refiner's fire" and "like a launderer's soap"—to describe the cleansing God will bring for his people.

• *Like a refiner's fire* (Mal. 3:2). One meaning of the word *refine* is to purify, as with an impure metal using heat or chemicals. In ancient times silver miners dug treasure from the ground. Because silver is an alloy metal, such miners almost always found silver in an impure form, mixed with other metals. The most ancient form of refining silver—a method silversmiths still use—is cupellation, which involves mixing silver with melted lead in a crucible (cupel) that goes into an extremely hot furnace. Such a refiner's fire melts the lead, absorbing it in the

45

crucible and leaving the pure silver in a ball. A silversmith may repeat this process several times to achieve absolute purity.

Someone once asked an old silversmith how he knew when to stop refining metal in the fire. "When I can see my face in it," he said. God promises to refine his people until he can "see his face" in them too—until they reflect his character.

- *Like a launderer's soap* (Mal. 3:2). If you've seen the movie *A Christmas Story*, you've seen what happens when Ralphie curses: his mom sticks a fresh bar of Lifebouy soap in his mouth. Eww! The soap serves as a picture of what Ralphie needs—a cleaner tongue. When my four siblings and I were little, if we used naughty language, my mother gave us similar treatment. There's nothing like the threat of a fat chunk of Irish Spring or Ivory to make a kid think twice about what flies out of his mouth!

The purpose of soap is to cleanse. And the tougher the stain, the harsher the treatment. When my dad gets his hands greasy working on the car, he doesn't wash with Lifebouy or Ivory. He pulls out the Lava, the heavy-duty cleaner that's like forty-grit sandpaper. And when I get a spaghetti-sauce stain on my starched cotton blouse, I take it to the cleaners, because they have the launderers' soap, the "soap on steroids" for treating serious stains and brightening fabric.

Through the two similes in Malachi 3:2, the refiner's fire and soap, God communicates in creative ways what he desires from his people: purified lives. In the future he promises a wholesale, national cleansing with fire and extra-strength soap. But in the meantime the Spirit works in individuals. Are you in the fire? Are you feeling the sandpaper-like soap? Submit your will to God. Ask him to grant you the grace to cooperate with his refining process so you might shine, purified and spotless.

MONDAY: THE COMING DAY

1. Pray for insight and read Malachi 3–4.

Malachi 3

3:1 "I am about to send my messenger, who will clear the way before me. Indeed, the Lord you are seeking will suddenly come to his temple, and the messenger of the covenant, whom you long for, is certainly coming," says the LORD who rules over all.

3:2 Who can endure the day of his coming? Who can keep standing when he appears? For he will be like a refiner's fire, like a launderer's soap. **3:3** He will act like a refiner and purifier of silver and will cleanse the Levites and refine them like gold and silver. Then they will offer the LORD a proper offering. **3:4** The offerings of Judah and Jerusalem will be pleasing to the LORD as in former times and years past.

3:5 "I will come to you in judgment. I will be quick to testify against those who practice divination, those who commit adultery, those who break promises, and those who exploit workers, widows, and orphans, who refuse to help the immigrant and in this way show they do not fear me," says the LORD who rules over all.

3:6 "Since, I, the LORD, do not go back on my promises, you, sons of Jacob, have not perished. **3:7** From the days of your ancestors you have ignored my commandments and have not kept them! Return to me, and I will return to you," says the LORD who rules over all. "But you say, 'How should we return?' **3:8** Can a person rob God? You indeed are robbing me, but you say, 'How are we robbing you?' In tithes and contributions! **3:9** You are bound for judgment because you are robbing me—this whole nation is guilty.

3:10 "Bring the entire tithe into the storehouse so that there may be food in my temple. Test me in this matter," says the LORD who rules over all, "to see if I will not open for you the windows of heaven and pour out for you a blessing until there is no room for it all. **3:11** Then I will stop the plague from ruining your crops, and the vine will not lose its fruit before harvest," says the LORD who rules over all. **3:12** "All nations will call you happy, for you indeed will live in a delightful land," says the LORD who rules over all.

3:13 "You have criticized me sharply," says the LORD, "but you ask, 'How have we criticized you?' **3:14** You have said, 'It is useless to serve God. How have we been helped by keeping his requirements and going about like mourners before the LORD who rules over all? **3:15** So now we consider the arrogant to be happy; indeed, those who practice evil are successful. In fact, those who challenge God escape!'"

3:16 Then those who respected the LORD spoke to one another, and the LORD took notice. A scroll was prepared before him in which were recorded the names of those who respected the LORD and honored his name. **3:17** "They will belong to me," says the LORD who rules over all, "in the day when I prepare my own special property.

I will spare them as a man spares his son who serves him. **3:18** Then once more you will see that I make a distinction between the righteous and the wicked, between the one who serves God and the one who does not.

Malachi 4

4:1 (3:19) "For indeed the day is coming, burning like a furnace, and all the arrogant evildoers will be chaff. The coming day will burn them up," says the Lord who rules over all. "It will not leave even a root or branch. **4:2** But for you who respect my name, the sun of vindication will rise with healing wings, and you will skip about like calves released from the stall. **4:3** You will trample on the wicked, for they will be like ashes under the soles of your feet on the day which I am preparing," says the Lord who rules over all.

4:4 "Remember the law of my servant Moses, to whom at Horeb I gave rules and regulations for all Israel to obey. **4:5** "Look, I will send you Elijah the prophet before the great and terrible day of the Lord arrives. **4:6** He will encourage fathers and their children to return to me, so that I will not come and strike the earth with judgment."

2. Describe God's concerns in this section of Malachi.

_____

_____

_____

3. Jews in the Second Temple period (516 BC–AD 70) had several expectations for the role of Messiah and the renewal of purity and righteousness. To understand what these were, we need to look briefly at history leading up to the ministry of Jesus.

When Antiochus IV Epiphanes desecrated the temple in Jerusalem in 167 BC by sacrificing swine on the altar, the Jews experienced the "abomination that causes desolation" (Dan. 9:27; quoted by Jesus in Matt. 24:15). This led Jewish patriots to revolt (the Maccabean revolt). They threw off the Seleucid (Greek) yoke. Three years later they cleansed and rededicated the temple. The word *Hanukkah* comes from the Hebrew word for *dedication*. The Maccabean temple dedication inaugurated a celebration of eight days, known to us as Hanukkah or the Feast of Dedication (John 10:22).

From 164 BC until 63 BC, the Jewish Hasmoneans ruled the land of Israel. Hasmonean is another name for the Maccabean descendants. Unfortunately, the Hasmoneans degenerated into corruption, and they oversaw a long period of political intrigue, religious compromise, assassinations, and small-scale civil war. The weakness of competing Jewish factions—the politically minded Sadducees, the scholarly Pharisees, the patriotic Zealots, and the ascetic and separatist Essenes—spurred the Romans to take advantage of their lack of unity, step in, and declare their rule under General Pompey in 63 BC.

Jesus was born during this time of Jewish impurity, when Palestine lived under the yoke of Roman occupation. While most Jews longed for a messianic figure to deliver them from Gentile oppression, they had no unified expectation for him. Some hoped for a kinglike political deliverer who would overthrow the Romans. Others looked for a high priest to restore the purity of the temple and the holiness of the priesthood. Still others longed for a prophet-messiah who would call the people as a nation back to repentance and holy living.

Jesus fulfilled all three messianic expectations. First, he came as the king of the Jews. He entered Jerusalem on a donkey as Solomon had done at his own coronation, and in the future Jesus will reign from the literal city of New Jerusalem. Second, Jesus was a priest who purified the temple. He bracketed his public ministry with two temple cleansings, both his first public act (John 2:13–22) and his last major public act (Matt. 21:12–17) were cleansings of the temple. Finally, Jesus was a prophet, speaking the word of the Lord.

The people in Malachi's day were looking for a prophet, priest, and king. Today we look back on history and see that the true Prophet-Priest-King has come. And he also fulfilled an even greater messianic role as the perfect God-man who died on the cross as the substitutionary atonement for the sins of the world.

How can you, with the Spirit's help, better obey God's words of warning and promise? How can you more faithfully come to Christ as your intermediary? How can you do homage to him as your king?

_____

_____

_____

_____

Tuesday: Taxes, Tithes, and Offerings

1. Pray for insight and read Malachi 3:5–9.

> **3:5** "I will come to you in judgment. I will be quick to testify against those who practice divination, those who commit adultery, those who break promises, and those who exploit workers, widows, and orphans, who refuse to help the immigrant, and in this way show they do not fear me," says the LORD who rules over all.
>
> **3:6** "Since, I, the LORD, do not go back on my promises, you, sons of Jacob, have not perished. **3:7** From the days of your ancestors you have ignored my commandments and have not kept them! Return to me, and I will return to you," says the LORD who rules over all. "But you say, 'How should we return?' **3:8** Can a person rob God? You indeed are robbing me, but you say, 'How are we robbing you?' In tithes and contributions! **3:9** You are bound for judgment because you are robbing me—this whole nation is guilty."

2. In the last chapter of Malachi, we saw that God refused to answer prayer because of the men's disregard for their marriage covenants. In this chapter, we find God addressing additional problems: how his people treated others, the fact that they were robbing from God, and their failure to fear God's name. What practices does God say offend him (3:5)?

_____

_____

_____

3. What do such practices reveal about one's view of God (3:5)?

_____

_____

_____

_____

4. Verse 6 seems to serve as a transition to the next concern God has. What do we learn about the character of God (3:6)? Why is this characteristic important in this context?

_____

_____

_____

5. God ties stinginess with offerings to their lack of relationship with him. What does he tell them to do, and how do they respond (3:7)?

_____

_____

_____

6. Notice God does not give relational advice for how to repent; he does not say "pray more" or "gather together more" or "hear the Word more." How does God answer, and what is the people's consequence (3:8)?

_____

_____

_____

• *Can a person rob God?* (3:8). God asks a rhetorical question that would generally evoke the obvious "No!" If God is all-powerful, all-knowing, and omnipresent, who could pull off a crime against him? Yet he insists that in a certain sense the people are committing a form of robbery. His accusation suggests that the possessions his people are withholding belong to him in the first place.

7. What does God call their lack of giving (3:8–9)? What two things were God's people withholding, and what is the difference between them?

_____

_____

_____

_____

8. According to theologian Dr. Don Sunukjian, God's people in Old Testament times gave more than 20 percent of their income to the Lord. Both taxes and offerings were included in this sum. Their giving also supported the temple workers. Tithes were 10 percent; offerings were over and above this amount. In the New Testament, God's people are not commanded to tithe but to give generously. How do you think Old Testament and New Testament giving should differ?

_____

_____

_____

9. Some have said that this passage teaches that if you do not give 10 percent to God, he will take it from you anyway. How might that be true? How might that not be true?

_____

_____

10. Do you think that if God's people gave as we should, that we should also get discounts on items we wish to buy, and our cars should break down less often than other people's? Explain your answer.

11. Imagine you live in a part of the world where your income is just above the international poverty line of about $1 per day. How might you respond to hearing that some people who make more than $25,000 per year feel they cannot afford to give?

WEDNESDAY: NOBODY LOVES THE WICKED

1. Pray for insight and read Malachi 3:10–18.

> **3:10** "Bring the entire tithe into the storehouse so that there may be food in my temple. Test me in this matter," says the LORD who rules over all, "to see if I will not open for you the windows of heaven and pour out for you a blessing until there is no room for it all. **3:11** Then I will stop the plague from ruining your crops, and the vine will not lose its fruit before harvest," says the LORD who rules over all. **3:12** "All nations will call you happy, for you indeed will live in a delightful land," says the LORD who rules over all.

3:13 "You have criticized me sharply," says the LORD, "but you ask, 'How have we criticized you?' **3:14** You have said, 'It is useless to serve God. How have we been helped by keeping his requirements and going about like mourners before the LORD who rules over all? **3:15** So now we consider the arrogant to be happy; indeed, those who practice evil are successful. In fact, those who challenge God escape!'"

3:16 Then those who respected the LORD spoke to one another, and the LORD took notice. A scroll was prepared before him in which were recorded the names of those who respected the LORD and honored his name. **3:17** "They will belong to me," says the LORD who rules over all, "in the day when I prepare my own special property. I will spare them as a man spares his son who serves him. **3:18** Then once more you will see that I make a distinction between the righteous and the wicked, between the one who serves God and the one who does not."

2. What two commands does God give in Malachi 3:10, and why does he issue them?

_____

_____

_____

_____

- *Bring the entire tithe into the storehouse* (3:10). Some have taught that when God told the people to bring their offerings "into the storehouse," he established a principle of giving to the local church first. While this may be a good priority, it is not at all what this text means. The storehouse was either the treasury of the temple of the Lord (see 1 Kings 7:51) or, in a more figurative sense, a place from which all of God's blessings proceeded. We find the word *treasury* eighty times in the Old Testament, but in only a few places is it connected to the divine storehouse. (If there is a modern equivalent to the temple, it is the heart of the believer, not the church building.) "Entire tithe" stresses the firstfruits of crops, shekels, and offerings, but it also includes time, work, talents, hobbies, emotions—the whole person and all he or she owed God.

3. What does God promise if his people obey (3:11)?

_____

_____

_____

• *Stop the plague from ruining your crops* (3:11). In the agrarian world of Malachi, people measured wealth primarily in terms of crops and livestock. They depended on the plants in their backyard to eat. God promises that he will "rebuke the devourer" (NASB), which probably refers to keeping locusts or agricultural disease from destroying what the people planted. Indirectly, God is promising to prosper his people.

4. What will be the ultimate outcome of the people's obedience followed by God's blessing (3:12)?

_____

_____

_____

5. Take inventory. Are you robbing God of anything? Is it your time? talent? resources? If so, what will you do, by his grace, to change that? And when?

_____

_____

_____

_____

_____

6. God has another accusation for his people. What has been their accusation about him (3:14–15)?

_____

_____

7. What does God say he values (3:16–18)? What does he say he will do for the righteous?

_____

_____

_____

8. What cause-and-effect relationships do you see here, and how do the conditions require faith?

_____

_____

_____

_____

9. The Israelites found it hard to give and to trust God. What situations make it difficult for you to give and to trust God? Write out a prayer asking him to help you obey in action and to remove from your heart all the obstacles to fully trusting and obeying him.

_____

_____

_____

_____

_____

Say the word *injustice* and it's easy to come up with examples. Here are a few that popped into my head.

- Pol Pot, Adolf Hitler, and Joseph Stalin—to name a few—made careers of murder on a massive scale.
- In India a missionary and his two small sons were set on fire and burned to death by people who hate Christianity.
- My brother-in-law was killed by a texting driver who later laughed about what he had done and lied to cover it up.
- Islamists drive Nigerian Christians from their homes on a regular basis.
- My friend lost six family members in the Rwandan genocide.
- An evil man spends a lifetime enslaving more than thirty thousand child soldiers, whom he trains to kill people, including their parents.
- The president of a company for which I once worked negotiated a merger than lined his pockets with cash but left more than five hundred employees without jobs.
- A pimp's lies about my taxi-driving friend left him sitting in prison.

1. What are some of the injustices in the world at large and in your own world that break your heart?

_____

_____

_____

_____

_____

2. Pray for insight and read Malachi 4:1–3.

> **4:1 (3:19)** "For indeed the day is coming, burning like a furnace, and all the arrogant evildoers will be chaff. The coming day will burn them up," says the one who rules over all. "It will not leave

Malachi 3:19 and 4:1 Are the Same Verse

Notice that the numbers on Malachi 3:19 and 4:1 mark the same verses. Starting with 4:1, English verse numbers differ from the verse numbers in the Hebrew text. The Hebrew text does not have a chapter 4 but instead has twenty-four verses in chapter 3. Here's why.

The original biblical texts—both Old and New Testaments—had no chapter or verse divisions. Chapter divisions and versification of the Bible occurred many hundreds of years after the original texts were written. This means that such divisions are not divinely inspired but serve as helpful human paratext (text placed alongside the biblical text). Chapter divisions and verse notations make it much easier to cite, compare, and share Scripture.

We do find Old Testament chapter and verse divisions in the oldest copies of the Hebrew canon. Scribes assigned them to the Hebrew Bible in the first century. These scribes placed marks at the beginning and end of paragraph divisions. They also made small marks to serve as full stops (our version of a period) to indicate where a reader should take a breath, since the texts were often read aloud. With the advent of the printing press, typesetters usually converted these marks into verses. There were some exceptions, however, and as a result some Hebrew and English versification differs. In the psalms, for example, the Hebrew text includes attribution (such as "A psalm of David") as a separate verse, whereas English versions such as the New American Standard Bible include such information as part of verse 1 in chapters where such attributions appear.

even a root or branch. **4:2** But for you who respect my name, the sun of vindication will rise with healing wings, and you will skip about like calves released from the stall. **4:3** You will trample on the wicked, for they will be like ashes under the soles of your feet on the day which I am preparing," says the LORD who rules over all.

3. What word pictures describe "the day" in this text? In this context, is the day of the Lord a joyous or a frightening day?

_____

_____

_____

_____

• *The day is coming* and *coming day* (4:1). Throughout Scripture we find the phrase "the day of the Lord" or "that day." (See especially Joel 2:30–31; Amos 5:18; Obad. 1:15; 2 Thess. 2:1–3.) For the unbeliever, the day of the Lord comes as a terrifying time of judgment, "like a furnace" in which "arrogant evildoers" burn like "chaff." Those who emphasize only God's love miss that the Scriptures say God is also just. The promise of a future day of judgment is intended to give the believer hope: your vindication is coming!

4. According to this passage, what characterizes the wicked (3:19/4:1) and what characterizes the righteous (4:2)? What is the destiny of the wicked (3:19/4:1)?

_____

_____

_____

_____

5. Why do you think the author described the heat as "like a furnace" rather than like a fire?

_____

_____

_____

• *You who respect my name* (4:2). The Lord speaks to a specific group, not to all people under the sun. What God seeks from his people is that they fear, revere, and respect him.

6. What promise does God make to those who respect his name (4:2–3)?

_____

_____

7. Those who fear God will receive a reward; those who disrespect God face judgment. So is God like a vending machine in which we place our obedience and receive a desired outcome? Is there always a clear cause-and-effect relationship between obedience and blessing? Explain your answer.

_____

_____

_____

_____

_____

_____

- *The sun of vindication will rise* (4:2). The word translated here as "vindication" is the Hebrew word we normally translate "righteousness." But the context points to a specific kind of righteousness, and that is vindication for God's people.

Some scholars believe the "sun of righteousness" is a promise of general blessing to all people. But the qualification before it ("you who respect my name") suggests this sun's blessing has limited scope. It is not to all people but only to those who revere God.

We can gain a better understanding of this passage by doing a quick survey of Scripture and looking for personifications of God as light. The psalmist wrote, "The LORD God is a sun and a shield" (Ps. 84:11 NASB), and Isaiah promised, "The Lord will be to you an everlasting light, and the God your glory. Your sun shall no more go down . . . for the Lord will be your everlasting light" (Isa. 60:19–20, NKJV). Jesus himself said, "I am the light of the world" (John 8:12). Looking back on Jesus' life, Luke wrote, "The Dayspring from on high has visited us, to give light to those who sit in darkness" (1:78–79, NKJV). And John the elder wrote, "God is light" (1 John 1:5). Here in Malachi it appears that the prophet has combined two figures of speech—personification (God as sun) and anthropomorphism (God as bird). The sun, or light, of righteousness, or vindication, will rise up on wings for those who fear God's name, a metaphorical way

Healing in His Wings

Interestingly, the word in the Hebrew translated "wings" is the word used for an edge or outer extremity, whether of a bird, an army, or a garment's border. In Mark 6:56 we read that people in the marketplace brought the sick to Jesus so they could touch the fringe of his cloak and be healed. The woman with the menstrual disorder touched the edge of Jesus' cloak and immediately her bleeding stopped (Luke 8:44). "The edge of his cloak" refers to the kraspedon, *the blue fringes on a Jewish man's garment that marked him as a law keeper (see Num. 15:37–41). The woman, and possibly all the sick whom people brought to Jesus, touched the part of his garment that indicated his ritual righteousness—and they were healed.*

of saying the day of the Lord will come as a time when God deals with the wicked and vindicates his people. In a world that hates what is good and persecutes God's people, light will arise and chase away darkness.

- *With healing wings* (4:2). The reference to a sun that will rise with healing wings is a prediction we connect with Christ's second coming. From the perspective of those who revere God, we equate with justice and healing the vindication that comes with judgment. When Christ returns to reign, the world can expect the government on his shoulders to be a just one, with fair laws and equity for all. And on an individual level, people will have *shalom*, the whole-person wellness God designed us to have. Consider how the love of Christ, which brought him to earth, will someday make all things right.

8. What will be the effect of this rising sun with healing wings on the people of God—how will they respond and what will they do (4:2)?

_____

_____

_____

_____

1. Pray for the Spirit to grant you insight to understand and apply Scripture. Then read Malachi 4:1–6.

> **4:1 (3:19)** "For indeed the day is coming, burning like a furnace, and all the arrogant evildoers will be chaff. The coming day will burn them up," says the LORD who rules over all. "It will not leave even a root or branch. **4:2** But for you who respect my name, the sun of vindication will rise with healing wings, and you will skip about like calves released from the stall. **4:3** You will trample on the wicked, for they will be like ashes under the soles of your feet on the day which I am preparing," says the LORD who rules over all.
>
> **4:4** "Remember the law of my servant Moses, to whom at Horeb I gave rules and regulations for all Israel to obey. **4:5** Look, I will send you Elijah the prophet before the great and terrible day of the LORD arrives. **4:6** He will encourage fathers and their children to return to me, so that I will not come and strike the earth with judgment."

2. Compare Malachi 3:1 and 4:5.

> **3:1** "I am about to send my messenger, who will clear the way before me. Indeed, the Lord you are seeking will suddenly come to his temple, and the messenger of the covenant, whom you long for, is certainly coming," says the LORD who rules over all.
>
> . . . .
>
> **4:5** Look, I will send you Elijah the prophet before the great and terrible day of the LORD arrives.

What similarities do you see between the two promises about the messenger?

_____

_____

_____

_____

Malachi in Handel's *Messiah*

"Thus Saith the Lord"	Mal. 3:1
"But Who May Abide the Day of His Coming?"	Mal. 3:2
"And He Shall Purify"	Mal. 3:3

3. Notice that the text says "Elijah the prophet" and not "Elijah the Tishbite" will come. Do you think there could be any significance to this subtle difference? Why or why not?

4. Read Luke 1:17 and Revelation 11:3–12.

Luke 1:17 And he will go as forerunner before the Lord in the spirit and power of Elijah, to turn the hearts of the fathers back to their children and the disobedient to the wisdom of the just, to make ready for the Lord a people prepared for him."

Revelation 11:3 And I will grant my two witnesses authority to prophesy for 1,260 days, dressed in sackcloth. **11:4** (These are the two olive trees and the two lampstands that stand before the Lord of the earth.) **11:5** If anyone wants to harm them, fire comes out of their mouths and completely consumes their enemies. If anyone wants to harm them, they must be killed this way. **11:6** These two have the power to close up the sky so that it does not rain during the time they are prophesying. They have power to turn the waters to blood and to strike the earth with every kind of plague whenever they want. **11:7** When they have completed their testimony, the beast that comes up from the abyss will make war on them and conquer them and kill them. **11:8** Their corpses will lie in the street of the great city that is symbolically called Sodom and Egypt, where their Lord was also crucified. **11:9** For three and a half days those from every people, tribe, nation, and language will look at their corpses, because they will not permit them to be placed in a tomb. **11:10** And those who live on the earth will rejoice over them and celebrate, even sending gifts to each other, because these two prophets had tormented those who live on the earth. **11:11** But after three and a half days a breath of life from God entered them, and they stood on their feet, and tremendous fear seized those who were watching them. **11:12** Then they heard a loud voice from heaven saying to them: "Come up here!" So the two prophets went up to heaven in a cloud while their enemies stared at them.

How do these two passages seem to tie in with our text from Malachi? Do you think it is possible that "Elijah" may be figurative here rather than literal? Why or why not?

_____

_____

_____

_____

5. What attitude toward God does Malachi 4 suggest God's followers should have?

_____

_____

_____

6. In Genesis we read that Hagar called God *El Roi,* "the God who sees." Because God sees all, he brings justice for his people. In this week's section of Malachi, we see promises made to the nation that God will someday restore justice. List circumstances in which it is hard for you to refrain from taking your own revenge in order to "make things right" and/or in which you long for God to bring about ultimate victory for you or those you love.

_____

_____

_____

_____

7. Malachi communicates a message of judgment against God's people. Yet how does it end?

_____

_____

_____

8. What does Malachi 4 teach us about God's character?

_____

_____

_____

9. Spend a few moments praying. Ask God to develop righteous character in you and to build your trust in him so that you can rely on his restorative justice to ultimately prevail. Express to God your hope for a future in which he will make all things new.

SATURDAY: RESTORATIVE JUSTICE

Scripture: "I will be quick to testify against those who practice divination, those who commit adultery, those who break promises, and those who exploit workers, widows, and orphans, who refuse to help the immigrant and in this way show they do not fear me," says the LORD who rules over all (Mal. 3:5).

My friend Célestin lost six family members, including his brother, in the Rwandan genocide. One day a man came to him to be baptized wearing a shirt Célestin recognized as having belonged to his own brother. When Célestin asked about it, the man said his relative had killed a man who wore it. Célestin was torn up inside, wanting to harm the man instead of baptizing him. But the Lord reminded Célestin that someone had died to give him newness of life.

Today Célestin and that man he baptized—the brother of his own brother's murderer—serve together as ministry partners. Célestin went on to write his doctoral dissertation on forgiveness, coauthor the book

Forgiving As We've Been Forgiven: Community Practices for Making Peace, and found ALARM—African Leadership and Reconciliation Ministry.

People often take *social justice* to mean the social gospel, which for many evokes connotations of all good works and no God. Certainly we do not attain salvation by our good works. We can add nothing to the work done for us on the cross by Jesus Christ. But the good news from on high actually does have social ramifications. When we follow God, it should make us different, not so we can earn his favor (one who knows Christ already has that) but to reflect that the Spirit has set us free and controls us. Notice in Malachi 3:5 that God expects the righteous to have certain characteristics. They are faithful to him, faithful to spouses, faithful to keep promises, fair to their workers, merciful to widows and orphans, and committed to helping immigrants.

In the Old Testament *righteousness* and *justice* are often the same word. And the sort of justice connected with righteousness is not about simply doling out a punishment someone deserves. It's about making right the wrong, which goes far beyond making the punishment fit the crime. It has an element of restoration.

That is why the term I prefer for this sort of whole-person approach is *restorative justice*. It requires more than punitive action such as a jail sentence. It requires restitution and reconciliation—a genuine demonstration of remorse with an apology and attempts to make wrongs right.

Each of us should be living out such justice, as it sets free both oppressed and oppressor. As I once heard author Shane Claiborne say, in addition to loving the poor, God also "loves the 1 percent rich who are suffering, though not suffering in the same ways as the poor, but they have high rates of loneliness, depression, and suicide." We are to emulate the one who preached "good news to the poor; set free the captives" (Luke 4:18), which by implication also includes the oppressors, who live in bondage to self. The Spirit frees both oppressed and oppressor.

Have you been completely faithful to God? Have you always affirmed marriage? Have you kept all your promises? Been completely unbiased with workers? Shown mercy to widows and orphans? Reached out to help immigrants? If not, repent and receive his grace. With his power you can be the kind of person who models the kind of righteousness God desires.

Have you suffered from injustice? Has someone broken promises to you? Has your spouse failed to uphold his vows? Has an employer mistreated you? Are you a widow or orphan or immigrant, lacking social power? Have you had to watch as someone you love endured a great injustice? If so, know that the just God, the one who rules over all, will someday right every wrong and make all things new.

Pray: Lord, have mercy on me for all the times I've failed to act justly, and defend me through times when I suffer injustice at the hands of others. I worship you, O God of grace and righteousness. I offer you my body, my mind, my love, my possessions, my time, my talents, my power, my potential, my spheres of influence. All that I have is yours and comes from you. Take and use all of me for your glory. In the name of Jesus, Amen.

Memorize: But for you who respect my name, the sun of vindication will rise with healing wings, and you will skip about like calves released from the stall (Mal. 4:2).

The Four Hundred Silent Years

Malachi forges a connecting link between the Old and New Testaments with its messianic prophecies. Four hundred years would pass before the last prophecies about the Messiah's first advent were fulfilled. Because no prophet's words were recorded as Scripture during this time, the intervening period is known as the four hundred silent years.

SUNDAY: REVERENCE IN SILENCE

Scripture: "I am about to send my messenger, who will clear the way before me. Indeed, the Lord you are seeking will suddenly come to his temple, and the messenger of the covenant, whom you long for, is certainly coming," says the LORD who rules over all (Mal. 3:1).

When I (Malia) was a child, my eight-year-old friend and I terrorized the poor babysitter my mom hired for the weekend while she took a much-deserved vacation. We left behind a trail of dirty dishes, from the living room to the kitchen, and we decorated the entire house with dress-up clothes. We watched that sitter scramble to clean up before my mom's return and didn't even lift a finger to help. Sadly, we didn't heed my mother's instruction to obey the sitter. While mom was gone, we disobeyed.

How do you act in the absence of authority? When your boss leaves for vacation, do you fudge your timecard? With no police in sight, do you roll through the stop sign? When it doesn't seem like he's watching, do you honor God with your hidden thoughts?

Malachi ends with a challenge to genuinely worship and obey God. Through his prophet's message, God challenged his people to love and revere him even in the absence of his word. During the four hundred years of quietude, God tested his people's faith. But Malachi also concludes with God's promise that he will speak again—through Messiah. God intended that the revelation of Messiah would draw his people back to their heavenly Father and motivate grateful worship. In preparation for God's gift of Messiah, the Lord promised to send his messenger to make his people ready.

This messenger, who would prepare Israel for Messiah by calling them to repentance, would show God's mercy and justice. The corrupt priesthood in Malachi's day mocked God's gift of grace and led the people to sin. They all faced God's judgment. Messiah's arrival would bring discipline to the corrupt religious leaders and restoration of true worship to the people.

Reread Malachi 3:1 and reflect on God's promise to send Messiah—Jesus Christ—who will reestablish righteousness and reveal grace. God sees everything and will one day make all things right.

> **3:1** "I am about to send my messenger, who will clear the way before me. Indeed, the Lord you are seeking will suddenly come to his temple, and the messenger of the covenant, whom you long for, is certainly coming," says the LORD who rules over all.

So how *do* you act when no one is watching? Remember—God sees everything. Examine your heart and ask God to reveal the areas of your life in which secret sin hides. Pray for forgiveness. God's unending grace—shown in his gift of his Son—covers every sin and restores your relationship with God.

1. Write about a time when God seemed silent to you. How did he help you to honor and trust him during that time?

_____

_____

_____

_____

_____

_____

2. Pray for insight and read Malachi 3:1-4.

> **3:1-4** "See, I will send my messenger, who will prepare the way before me. Then suddenly the Lord you are seeking will come to his temple; the messenger of the covenant, whom you desire, will come," says the LORD Almighty. But who can endure the day of his coming? Who can stand when he appears? For he will be like a refiner's fire or a launderer's soap. He will sit as a refiner and purifier of silver; he will purify the Levites and refine them like gold and silver. Then the LORD will have men who will bring offerings in righteousness, and the offerings of Judah and Jerusalem will be acceptable to the LORD, as in days gone by, as in former years."

3. Based on Malachi 3:1-4, what kind of gifts or offerings does God desire?

_____

_____

_____

4. In light of Messiah's future return (as described in Mark 14:62), what kind of gifts do you want to give to God?

_____

_____

_____

5. Write out a prayer asking God to help you to worship him and treasure the gift of Jesus Christ

_____

_____

_____

_____

To understand the chaotic years between Malachi's message and Messiah's advent, let's take a brief look at this period.

Israel during the 400 Silent Years	
Events In Israel/Palestine	Approximate Time Period
Persians rule	539–334 BC
Malachi prophesies	432–425 BC
Greeks rule (Alexander the Great)	334–323 BC
Alexander's generals rule and compete for power	323–301 BC
Ptolemies rule	301–200 BC
Seleucids rule	200–165 BC
Hasmonaeans rule (allowing Jewish autonomy)	165–40 BC
Romans rule (Herod the Great)	40–4 BC

When Malachi shared God's message with his people, Israel existed as a vassal state; the nation had limited power under the sovereign authority of the Persian king. During this time, Cyrus, the Persian ruler, gave a measure of independent rule to the Jewish priests. But the priests were corrupt, so they displeased God and triggered his discipline—his silence. The Hebrew Bible doesn't describe the actions of his people during the silent years before Messiah's arrival. But God's Word does foretell the changing Gentile power structure during this period.

Years earlier, the book of Daniel foretold the succession of Gentile empires that would rule over Israel. Daniel predicted the rise of the Greek Empire under the young leader Alexander the Great and the division of his empire among his generals after his untimely death. We read this prediction in chapter 11 of Daniel's prophecy.

6. Pray for insight and read Daniel 11:1–38.

11:1 And in the first year of Darius the Mede, I stood to strengthen him and to provide protection for him.) **11:2** Now I will tell you the truth.

Three more kings will arise for Persia. Then a fourth king will be unusually rich, more so than all who preceded him. When he has amassed power through his riches, he will stir up everyone against the kingdom of Greece. **11:3** Then a powerful king will arise, exercising great authority and doing as he pleases. **11:4** Shortly after his rise to power, his kingdom will be broken up and distributed toward the four winds of the sky—but not to his posterity or with the authority he exercised, for his kingdom will be uprooted and distributed to others besides these.

11:5 Then the king of the south and one of his subordinates will grow strong. His subordinate will resist him and will rule a kingdom greater than his. **11:6** After some years have passed, they will form an alliance. Then the daughter of the king of the south will come to the king of the north to make an agreement, but she will not retain her power, nor will he continue in his strength. She, together with the one who brought her, her child, and her benefactor will all be delivered over at that time.

11:7 There will arise in his place one from her family line who will come against their army and will enter the stronghold of the king of the north and will move against them successfully. **11:8** He will also take their gods into captivity to Egypt, along with their cast images and prized utensils of silver and gold. Then he will withdraw for some years from the king of the north. **11:9** Then the king of the north will advance against the empire of the king of the south, but will withdraw to his own land. **11:10** His sons will wage war, mustering a large army which will advance like an overflowing river and carrying the battle all the way to the enemy's fortress.

11:11 Then the king of the south will be enraged and will march out to fight against the king of the north, who will also muster a large army, but that army will be delivered into his hand. **11:12** When the army is taken away, the king of the south will become arrogant. He will be responsible for the death of thousands and thousands of people, but he will not continue to prevail. **11:13** For the king of the north will again muster an army, one larger than before. At the end of some years he will advance with a huge army and enormous supplies.

11:14 In those times many will oppose the king of the south. Those who are violent among your own people will rise up in confirmation of the vision, but they will falter. **11:15** Then the king of the north will advance and will build siege mounds and capture a well-fortified city. The forces of the south will not prevail, not even his finest contingents. They will have no strength to prevail. **11:16** The one advancing against him will do as he pleases, and no one will be able to stand before him. He will prevail in the beautiful land, and its annihilation will be within his power. **11:17** His intention will be to come with the strength of his entire kingdom, and he will form alliances. He will give the king of the south a daughter in marriage in order to destroy the kingdom, but it will not turn out to his advantage. **11:18** Then he will turn his attention to the coastal regions and will capture many of them. But a commander will bring his shameful conduct to a halt; in addition, he will make him pay for his shameful conduct. **11:19** He will then turn his attention to the fortresses of his own land, but he will stumble and fall, not to be found again. **11:20** There will arise after him one who will send out an exactor of tribute to enhance the splendor of the kingdom, but after a few days he will be destroyed, though not in anger or battle.

11:21 Then there will arise in his place a despicable person to whom the royal honor has not been rightfully conferred. He will come on the scene in a time of prosperity and will seize the kingdom through deceit. **11:22** Armies will be suddenly swept away in defeat before him; both they and a covenant leader will be destroyed. **11:23** After entering into an alliance with him, he will behave treacherously; he will ascend to power with only a small force. **11:24** In a time of prosperity for the most productive areas of the province he will come and accomplish what neither his fathers nor their fathers accomplished. He will distribute loot, spoils, and property to his followers, and he will devise plans against fortified cities, but not for long. **11:25** He will rouse his strength and enthusiasm against the king of the south with a large army. The king of the south will wage war with a large and very powerful army, but he will not be able to prevail because of the plans devised against him. **11:26** Those who share the king's fine food will attempt to destroy him, and his army will be swept away; many will be killed in battle. **11:27** These two kings, their minds filled with evil intentions, will trade lies with one another at the same table. But it will not succeed, for there is still an end at the appointed time. **11:28** Then the king of the north will return to his own land with much property. His mind will be set against the holy covenant. He will take action, and then return to his own land. **11:29** At an appointed time he will again invade the south, but this latter visit will not turn out the way the former one did. **11:30** The ships of Kittim will come against him, leaving him disheartened. He will turn back and direct his indignation against the holy covenant. He will return and honor those who forsake the holy covenant. **11:31** His forces will rise up and profane the fortified sanctuary, stopping the daily sacrifice. In its place they will set up the abomination that causes desolation. **11:32** Then with smooth words he will defile those who have rejected the covenant. But the people who are loyal to their God will act valiantly. **11:33** These who are wise among the people will teach the masses. However, they will fall by the sword and by the flame, and they will be imprisoned and plundered for some time. **11:34** When they stumble, they will be granted some help. But many will unite with them deceitfully. **11:35** Even some of the wise will stumble, resulting in their refinement, purification, and cleansing until the time of the end, for it is still for the appointed time.

11:36 Then the king will do as he pleases. He will exalt and magnify himself above every deity and he will utter presumptuous things against the God of gods. He will succeed until the time of wrath is completed, for what has been decreed must occur. **11:37** He will not respect the gods of his fathers—not even the god loved by women. He will not respect any god; he will elevate himself above them all. **11:38** What he will honor is a god of fortresses—a god his fathers did not acknowledge he will honor with gold, silver, valuable stones, and treasured commodities."

• *The kings of the north* (multiple references) were the rulers in Syria. The specific king mentioned in verses 21–35 is Antiochus IV Epiphanes, who persecuted the Jews and polluted the temple.

- *The kings of the south* (multiple references) were the rulers in Egypt, known as the Ptolemaic dynasty.

7. What does this chapter indicate about God's sovereignty?

_____

_____

_____

8. How did God expect his people to live during this tumultuous period in history?

_____

_____

9. Were God's expectations then any different from what he expects today? Explain your answer.

_____

_____

_____

TUESDAY: DO YOU HEAR WHAT I HEAR?

1. Look back on your reading from Daniel yesterday. How did the kings of the north and south exercise their sovereignty? Did they honor God?

_____

_____

_____

2. According to Daniel's prophecy, who really wielded power?

_____

3. How do you use the sovereignty you have received from God in your family, your work, and your relationships?

_____

_____

_____

_____

_____

Do you ever feel like God is silent when you want him to speak? Does it seem like he gives you the cold shoulder when you need to hear from him most? After college, I experienced God's silence. I looked toward the future and didn't know what career path to follow, and I needed to hear his voice, but he remained silent. Or was he? In the midst of his quietude, God gave me a desire to read his Word.

We may not have modern-day prophets like Malachi who disclose new words from God or reveal history before it happens. We have something better! God continues to speak through his inspired, perfect Word. And Christians today have received the gift of the indwelling Holy Spirit—the third person of the Trinity—from the Father and the Son. The Spirit enables us to read the Bible and understand God's voice (see John 14:15–26).

4. Pray and thank God for giving us his trustworthy Word and ask the Spirit to grant insight. Then read Psalm 19:7–14.

> **19:7** The law of the LORD is perfect
> and preserves one's life.
> The rules set down by the LORD are reliable
> and impart wisdom to the inexperienced.
> **19:8** The LORD's precepts are fair
> and make one joyful.
> The LORD's commands are pure
> and give insight for life.

19:9 The commands to fear the LORD are right
and endure forever.
The judgments given by the LORD are trustworthy
and absolutely just.
19:10 They are of greater value than gold,
than even a great amount of pure gold;
they bring greater delight than honey,
than even the sweetest honey from a honeycomb.
19:11 Yes, your servant finds moral guidance there;
those who obey them receive a rich reward.
19:12 Who can know all his errors?
Please do not punish me for sins I am unaware of.
19:13 Moreover, keep me from committing flagrant sins;
do not allow such sins to control me.
Then I will be blameless,
and innocent of blatant rebellion.
19:14 May my words and my thoughts
be acceptable in your sight,
O LORD, my sheltering rock and my redeemer.

5. How does this passage say God's Word benefits his people?

_____

_____

_____

_____

_____

6. Do you treasure the gift of God's Word? If so, how?

_____

_____

_____

7. Persia, Greece, Egypt, Syria, and Rome ruled over Israel during the four hundred years of silence before the arrival of Messiah. Israel lived with the memory of God's voice mixed with the voices of the pagan nations that had dominated them. The historical text below describes two kinds of Jews who lived during the time between the Old and New Testaments—those who trusted in God's love and those who deserted him to chase idols. Read the following excerpt from the first-century Jewish historian Josephus in *Antiquities of the Jews*. As Josephus describes his people during the intertestamental period, pay attention to how he describes Israel's attitude toward God. (You can find the entire account in *Antiquities* 12:246–257).

> [246] King Antiochus returning out of Egypt for fear of the Romans, made an expedition against the city of Jerusalem; [247] And when he had gotten possession of Jerusalem, he slew many of the opposite party; and when he had plundered it of a great deal of money, he returned to Antioch. . . . [253] And when the king had built an idol altar upon God's altar, he slew swine upon it, and so offered a sacrifice neither according to the Law, nor the Jewish religious worship in that country. He also compelled them to forsake the worship which they paid their own God, and to adore those whom he took to be gods; and made them build temples, and raise idol altars in every city and village, and offer swine upon them every day. [254] He also commanded them not to circumcise their sons, and threatened to punish any that should be found to have transgressed his injunction. [255] And, indeed, many Jews there were who complied with the king's commands, either voluntarily, or out of fear of the penalty that was pronounced. But the best men, and those of the noblest souls, did not regard him, but did pay a greater respect to the customs of their country than concern as to the punishment which he threatened to the disobedient; on which account they every day underwent great miseries and bitter torments.

Summarize how Josephus describes those who obeyed the Mosaic law.

Ancient historians such as Josephus and Pausanias provide historical glimpses of life under Roman rule from the first century BC to the second century AD. Another source for information about this time is the Apocrypha. In the Apocrypha, for example, we learn about Hanukkah, or the Feast of Dedication, that Jesus attended (John 10:22–39).

The Apocrypha (from the Greek word for "hidden") refers to a selection of ancient writings sometimes included between the Old and New Testaments in modern English Bibles. These include fourteen or fifteen books—depending on the translation—including 1 and 2 Esdras, Tobit, Judith, Rest of Esther, Wisdom, Ecclesiasticus (not to be confused with the Book of Ecclesiastes), Baruch, The Epistle of Jeremy, Song of the Three Children, Story of Susanna, Bel and the Dragon, Prayer of Manasses, and 1 and 2 Maccabees.

While some of these books are considered to be Scripture, or canonical—and thus divinely authoritative—by the Catholic Church (so affirmed by the Council of Trent in 1546), all of them are considered noncanonical (nonauthoritative) by Protestants (so confirmed by the Westminster Confession in 1647).

How did Protestants decide what books are canonical?

The Hebrew and Aramaic biblical canon, the Old Testament, was more or less accepted by the time of Jesus, who himself seemed to endorse the biblical canon of his day. For instance, when Jesus said that the Pharisees would be guilty of all the righteous blood that had been shed from the time of Abel through Zechariah (Matt. 23:35), he was referring to the first (Genesis) and last (2 Chronicles) books of the Hebrew canon, thus tacitly endorsing the Old Testament's validity as an entire and comprehensive body of material.

For the New Testament canon, books had to pass several criteria:

- apostolicity (written or endorsed by an apostle)
- universality of acceptance by the church, and
- complete consistency with other biblical writings.

Because Protestants do not consider the apocryphal books as divinely inspired Scripture, one might think it is wrong to quote them here. Is it okay to use them? The answer to that question depends on *how* we might use them. Here are three reasons for us to use them as sources:

- Though the books are not considered authoritative Scripture, many of them contain wise sayings by godly people that have value just as any truth has value. "All truth is God's truth."

Think of how many books we read by wise people that are not Scripture but help to guide our lives.

- The books have historical value. For example, 1 and 2 Maccabees contain historical material about the Maccabean revolt and Hasmonean rule that scholars would not otherwise know about. Included is the story of the temple rededication, celebrated later as the Feast of Dedication, which Jesus himself observed.
- The New Testament itself includes a quotation from at least one noncanonical book (Jude quotes *The Book of Enoch* 14–15), demonstrating that while the Bible contains sufficient truth, it does not contain exhaustive truth.

In this week's study you will find quotes from extrabiblical sources. These we have set in a different typeface to identify them. But you will also see that each day your study includes at least one Bible reading.

8. Spend time thanking God that after four hundred years he broke his silence and that you are a blessed recipient of his "Word made flesh."

WEDNESDAY: WORTHLESS PRESENTS

A nation is only as good as its leaders. If leaders abandon morality and justice, so will the people. Many of the priests during and after Malachi's time continued to live in hypocrisy throughout the silent years. They practiced their religious rituals but failed to allow God's law to penetrate their righteous facades. They gave the sovereign, gracious God who rules over all their beautifully wrapped boxes filled with foul-smelling garbage. Centuries earlier God had spoken through the prophet Isaiah to communicate the kind of worship he desires.

1. Pray for insight and read about how God rejected the empty worship of the priests (Isaiah 1:11–17).

> **1:11** "Of what importance to me are your many sacrifices?"
> says the LORD.
> "I am stuffed with burnt sacrifices
> of rams and the fat from steers.
> The blood of bulls, lambs, and goats
> I do not want.
> **1:12** When you enter my presence,

do you actually think I want this—
animals trampling on my courtyards?
1:13 Do not bring any more meaningless offerings;
I consider your incense detestable!
You observe new moon festivals, Sabbaths, and convocations,
but I cannot tolerate sin-stained celebrations!
1:14 I hate your new moon festivals and assemblies;
they are a burden
that I am tired of carrying.
1:15 When you spread out your hands in prayer,
I look the other way;
when you offer your many prayers,
I do not listen,
because your hands are covered with blood.
1:16 Wash! Cleanse yourselves!
Remove your sinful deeds
from my sight.
Stop sinning!
1:17 Learn to do what is right!
Promote justice!
Give the oppressed reason to celebrate!
Take up the cause of the orphan!
Defend the rights of the widow!

The heartless ritualism among many priests continued from the time of Isaiah through the years before Messiah's arrival. But when persecution came, the priests and the people had to make a choice—forsake the law to avoid persecution or worship God from the heart, regardless of the consequences.

Alexander the Great's top military generals fought for supremacy after his death in 323 BC, and in the process they splintered the Greek Empire. In 137 BC, Antiochus IV Epiphanes, one of the Syrian rulers, came to power and terrorized the Jews. You already read in Josephus's account about what he did. The prophet Daniel had predicted Antiochus's abominable, idolatrous practices.

2. Pray for insight and reread Daniel 11:21–35.

11:21 "Then there will arise in his place a despicable person to whom the royal honor has not been rightfully conferred. He will come on the scene in a time of prosperity and will seize the kingdom through deceit. **11:22** Armies will be suddenly swept away in defeat before him; both they and a covenant leader will be destroyed. **11:23** After entering into an alliance with him, he will behave treacherously; he will ascend to power with only a small force. **11:24** In a time of prosperity for the most productive areas of the province he will come and accomplish what neither his fathers nor their fathers accomplished. He will distribute loot, spoils, and property to his followers, and he will devise plans against fortified cities, but not for long. **11:25** He will rouse his strength and enthusiasm against the king of the south with a large army.

The king of the south will wage war with a large and very powerful army, but he will not be able to prevail because of the plans devised against him. **11:26** Those who share the king's fine food will attempt to destroy him, and his army will be swept away; many will be killed in battle. **11:27** These two kings, their minds filled with evil intentions, will trade lies with one another at the same table. But it will not succeed, for there is still an end at the appointed time. **11:28** Then the king of the north will return to his own land with much property. His mind will be set against the holy covenant. He will take action, and then return to his own land. **11:29** At an appointed time he will again invade the south, but this latter visit will not turn out the way the former one did. **11:30** The ships of Kittim will come against him, leaving him disheartened. He will turn back and direct his indignation against the holy covenant. He will return and honor those who forsake the holy covenant. **11:31** His forces will rise up and profane the fortified sanctuary, stopping the daily sacrifice. In its place they will set up the abomination that causes desolation. **11:32** Then with smooth words he will defile those who have rejected the covenant. But the people who are loyal to their God will act valiantly. **11:33** These who are wise among the people will teach the masses. However, they will fall by the sword and by the flame, and they will be imprisoned and plundered for some time. **11:34** When they stumble, they will be granted some help. But many will unite with them deceitfully. **11:35** Even some of the wise will stumble, resulting in their refinement, purification, and cleansing until the time of the end, for it is still for the appointed time.

3. Describe the character of Antiochus Epiphanes—the dreaded "king of the north."

_____

_____

4. How did the king of the north treat the Jews who kept the holy covenant, the law of Moses (11:28–35)?

_____

_____

5. How did Antiochus Ephipanes treat the Jews who abandoned God's law and adopted Greek religion and culture?

_____

_____

_____

6. How did the righteous Jews respond to the king of the north and his godless policies?

_____

_____

Daniel 11:21–35 describes the emergence of two parties within the Jewish religious establishment—the Pharisees and the Sadducees. The Pharisees sought separation from Greek religion and culture. The Sadducees embraced and adopted Hellenistic ways. The Pharisees strove to keep the Mosaic law with precision and holiness. As a result, Antiochus Epiphanes persecuted them. The Sadducees, on the other hand, made a covenant with the evil king of the north. We read about Antiochus Ephiphanes in the apocryphal book of 1 Maccabees.

7. Read 1 Maccabees 1:10–15. (From the New American Bible [NAB], not to be confused with the New American Standard Bible [NASB])

> **1:10** There sprang from these a sinful offshoot, Antiochus Epiphanes, son of King Antiochus, once a hostage at Rome. He became king in the year one hundred and thirty-seven of the kingdom of the Greeks. 11 In those days there appeared in Israel men [Sadducees] who were breakers of the law, and they seduced many people, saying: 'Let us go and make an alliance with the Gentiles all around us; since we

separated from them, many evils have come upon us.' 12 The proposal was agreeable; 13 some from among the people promptly went to the king, and he authorized them to introduce the way of living of the Gentiles. 14 Thereupon they built a gymnasium in Jerusalem according to the Gentile custom. 15 They covered over the mark of their circumcision and abandoned the holy covenant; they allied themselves with the Gentiles and sold themselves to wrongdoing.

8. How did the Sadducees respond to the pagan rule of Antiochus Epiphanes?

_____

_____

9. Why do you think they allied with him and abandoned the holy covenant?

_____

_____

10. What aspects of our culture entice God's people to sin against our Lord?

_____

_____

_____

_____

11. In what ways are you guilty of conforming to culture over following God?

_____

_____

_____

During the time of Malachi, priests ruled the religious and political affairs of the Jews. This rule continued to some extent throughout the silent years. While God condemned the corrupt, inwardly calloused priests of Malachi's day, many faithful Jews obeyed God between the testaments. They sought holiness, pure worship, and separation from the Hellenizing forces of the Greek Empire. And they led others in the same devotion to God.[1]

During the time when Antiochus Epiphanes wreaked havoc on God's people, one brave Jewish woman watched as six of her seven sons were tortured and martyred before her eyes. When her last remaining son, her youngest, faced the choice to worship Greek idols or remain true to God, she rejoiced in his choice and encouraged him to stand firm.

1. Read 2 Maccabees 7:27–30 and 1 Maccabees 1:57–63 (NAB):

> **7:27** She leaned over close to her son and said in their native language: **7:28** "Son, have pity on me, who carried you in my womb for nine months, nursed you for three years, brought you up, educated and supported you to your present age. I beg you, child, to look at the heavens and the earth and see all that is in them; then you will know that God did not make them out of existing things; and in the same way the human race came into existence. **7:29** Do not be afraid of this executioner, but be worthy of your brothers and accept death, so that in the time of mercy I may receive you again with them." **7:30** She had scarcely finished speaking when the youth said: "What are you waiting for? I will not obey the king's command. I obey the command of the law given to our forefathers through Moses."
>
> **1 Maccabees 1:57** (NAB)—whoever observed the law, was condemned to death by royal decree. **1:58** So they used their power against Israel, against those who were caught, each month, in the cities. **1:59** On the twenty-fifth day of each month they sacrificed on the altar erected over the altar of holocausts. **1:60** Women who had had their children circumcised were put to death, in keeping with the decree, **1:61** with the babies hung from their necks; their fami-

---

1 H. A. Ironside, *The Four Hundred Silent Years: From Malachi to Matthew* (New York, NY: Loizeaux Brothers, Bible Truth Depot, 1914), 42–44.

lies also and those who had circumcised them were killed. **1:62** But many in Israel were determined and resolved in their hearts not to eat anything unclean; **1:63** they preferred to die rather than to be defiled with unclean food or to profane the holy covenant; and they did die. Terrible affliction was upon Israel.

2. List the commandments from the law of Moses that Antiochus Epiphanes prohibited and the punishment rendered on those who obeyed the law (vv. 57–63).

Commandment from the Law	Punishment

3. In the midst of war and political uncertainty, how did the faithful Jews react?

_____

_____

_____

_____

4. How did these faithful people demonstrate they were listening to God's voice in the midst of terror?

_____

_____

_____

5. What can we learn from their example of devotion to God?

_____

_____

_____

Not only did many Jews set themselves apart to God inwardly, but they sought the one to come—Messiah. As God's people faced the tidal wave of Roman occupation, they yearned for the promised Davidic king. Many writings during the last years of the Hasmonean period voiced the messianic hope. One such writing known as the Psalms of Solomon proclaims this expectation.

6. Read the Psalms of Solomon 17:21–27.

> **Psalms of Solomon 17:21–27** (Crandall)—21 "Behold, O Lord, and raise up unto them their king, the son of David, at the time known to you, O God, in order that he may reign over Israel your servant. 22 And gird him with strength, that he may shatter unrighteous rulers, and that he may purge Jerusalem from gentiles who trample (her) down to destruction. 23 Wisely, righteously he shall thrust out sinners from (the) inheritance; he shall destroy the arrogance of the sinner as a potter's jar. 24 With a rod of iron he shall shatter all their substance; he shall destroy the godless nations with the word of his mouth. 25 At his rebuke nations shall flee before him, and he shall reprove sinners for the thoughts of their heart. 26 And he shall gather together a holy people, whom he shall lead in righteousness, and he shall judge the tribes of the people who has been made holy by the Lord his God. 27 And he shall not suffer unrighteousness to lodge any more in their midst, nor shall there dwell with them any man who knows wickedness, for he shall know them, that they are all sons of their God.

7. For what does the author of this paragraph long?

_____

_____

_____

8. What does he hate about the Gentile rulers?

_____

_____

_____

_____

_____

9. Compare Jesus Christ as he is described in Revelation 19 with the Gentile lords described previously.

> **19:11** NET—Then I saw heaven opened and here came a white horse! The one riding it was called "Faithful" and "True," and with justice he judges and goes to war. **19:12** His eyes are like a fiery flame and there are many diadem crowns on his head. He has a name written that no one knows except himself. **19:13** He is dressed in clothing dipped in blood, and he is called the Word of God. **19:14** The armies that are in heaven, dressed in white, clean, fine linen, were following him on white horses. **19:15** From his mouth extends a sharp sword, so that with it he can strike the nations. He will rule them with an iron rod, and he stomps the winepress of the furious wrath of God, the All-Powerful. **19:16** He has a name written on his clothing and on his thigh: "King of kings and Lord of lords."

10. In what ways does the passage from Psalms of Solomon reflect God's values as we saw them in the Book of Malachi?

_____

_____

_____

_____

_____

11. What can we learn from the faithful people in Malachi's day who sought to honor God in the midst of persecution?

_____

_____

_____

12. What kind of gifts do you want to give to God? List what genuine gifts you can offer that arise from a heart of reverence and worship.

_____

_____

_____

13. In what ways can you share the true gift of Jesus Christ, the King of kings and Lord of lords, with your loved ones?

_____

_____

_____

FRIDAY: FIRST, ELIJAH MUST COME

In countries that celebrate Christmas, many preparations precede the presents, right? Think about the ads for Christmas dinner foods, decorations in the mall and on city streets, lights and wreaths on homes, ads for shopping, shopping, shopping, and the hunt for those perfect gifts. Christmas preparations persist until the long-expected morning. Likewise, before Messiah's advent, God sent his messenger so the people would prepare their hearts for his gift.

Now that we understand the turbulent period before Jesus Christ's arrival, let's think about how we can honor and obey God as we prepare to receive him daily, beyond our initial belief in Christ as

Lord. Let's focus on the Father's gift of the Son to us and the gifts of gratitude we should offer in return.

1. Pray for insight and read Malachi 4:4–6.

> **4:4** "Remember the law of Moses My servant, even the statutes and ordinances which I commanded him in Horeb for all Israel. **5** Behold, I am going to send you Elijah the prophet before the coming of the great and terrible day of the LORD. **6** He will restore the hearts of the fathers to their children and the hearts of the children to their fathers, so that I will not come and smite the land with a curse" (NASB).

- *Horeb* (4:4). Horeb is a mountain range; one of its summits is Mount Sinai. Today the range is known as Jebel Musa. At this location God gave the law to Moses; then when Moses descended, he discovered the people had given Aaron their ornaments to melt to create a golden calf for them to worship. A sampling of Bible verses about Horeb follows.

> **Exodus 3:1** Now Moses was shepherding the flock of his father-in-law Jethro, the priest of Midian, and he led the flock to the far side of the desert and came to the mountain of God, to Horeb.

> **Exodus 33:6** So the Israelites stripped off their ornaments by Mount Horeb.

> **Deuteronomy 5:2** The LORD our God made a covenant with us at Horeb.

> **Psalm 106:19** They made an image of a calf at Horeb, and worshiped a metal idol.

> **Deuteronomy 9:8** At Horeb you provoked him and he was angry enough with you to destroy you.

> **Deuteronomy 4:15** Be very careful, then, because you saw no form at the time the LORD spoke to you at Horeb from the middle of the fire.

> **Deuteronomy 29:1** These are the words of the covenant that the Lord commanded Moses to make with the people of Israel in the land of Moab, in addition to the covenant he had made with them at Horeb.

1 Kings 8:9 There was nothing in the ark except the two stone tablets Moses had placed there in Horeb. It was there that the LORD made an agreement with the Israelites after he brought them out of the land of Egypt.

Deuteronomy 4:10 You stood before the LORD your God at Horeb and he said to me, "Assemble the people before me so that I can tell them my commands. Then they will learn to revere me all the days they live in the land, and they will instruct their children."

Deuteronomy 18:16 This accords with what happened at Horeb in the day of the assembly. You asked the LORD your God: "Please do not make us hear the voice of the LORD our God any more or see this great fire any more lest we die."

2. Just as God had sent Moses to his people, he promised to send a messenger. Describe Elijah's role as laid out in Malachi 4:4–6.

_____

_____

_____

3. How does Elijah's message fulfill the purpose of the law of Moses?

_____

_____

_____

4. As we explore the role of the messenger, we gain insight from reading Matthew 3:1–11.

3:1 "Now in those days John the Baptist came, preaching in the wilderness of Judea, saying, **2** 'Repent, for the kingdom of heaven is at hand.' **3** For this is the one referred to by Isaiah the prophet when he said, 'THE VOICE OF ONE CRYING IN THE WILDERNESS, "MAKE READY THE WAY OF THE LORD, MAKE HIS PATHS STRAIGHT!"' **4** Now John himself had a garment of camel's hair and a leather belt around his waist; and his food was locusts and wild honey. **5** Then Jerusalem was going out to him, and all Judea and all the district around the Jordan; **6** and they were being baptized by him in the Jordan River, as they confessed their sins. **7** But when he saw many of the Pharisees and Sadducees coming for baptism, he said to them, 'You brood of vipers, who warned you to flee from the wrath to come? **8** Therefore bear fruit in keeping with repentance; **9** and do not suppose that you can say to yourselves, "We have Abraham for our father"; for I say to you that from these stones God is able to raise up children to Abraham. **10** The axe is already laid at the root of the trees; therefore every tree that does not bear good fruit is cut down and thrown into the fire. **11** As for me, I baptize you with water for repentance, but He who is coming after me is mightier than I, and I am not fit to remove His sandals; He will baptize you with the Holy Spirit and fire.'"

It's important to understand the role of Elijah. God didn't raise Elijah the prophet from the dead and send him to Israel before Jesus Christ's ministry. "Elijah" refers to the office of prophet. Just as Elijah prepared the way for Elisha's message of judgment (1 Kings 17–2 Kings 13), John the Baptist preached repentance prior to Jesus Christ's condemnation of the corrupt priesthood.

5. Identify Elijah in Malachi 4:4–5. Who was he?

_____

_____

6. What message did Elijah preach?

_____

_____

7. How did Elijah prepare the way for Messiah, and why was his ministry essential? (See Malachi 3:1–2.)

_____

_____

_____

For my college graduation, my mom surprised me with a wonderful gift—a beautiful new violin. I could do nothing for her to repay her for the generous present, especially since I lacked a job and money. All I could do to show my gratitude was honor her, thank her, show her my love, and tell all my friends about her amazing kindness.

In the same way that I could not repay my mother for her gift, none of us can repay God for the gift of his Son to our dark, sin-stained world. In light of God's unspeakable gift, how should we respond?

My favorite Christmas hymn, written by Charles Wesley, captures the awe-inspiring advent of Jesus Christ, the promised Messiah. The third stanza contains an allusion from Malachi. Read the words carefully and worshipfully.

Hark, the herald angels sing, "Glory to the newborn King:
Peace on earth, and mercy mild, God and sinner reconciled!"
Joyful, all ye nations rise, Join the triumph of the skies;
With the angelic host proclaim, "Christ is born in Bethlehem!"
Hark, the herald angels sing, "Glory to the newborn King."

Christ, by highest heavens adored; Christ, the everlasting Lord!
Late in time behold Him come, Offspring of the virgin's womb.
Veiled in flesh the Godhead see; Hail the incarnate Deity.
Pleased as man with men to dwell, Jesus, our Emmanuel.
Hark, the herald angels sing, "Glory to the newborn King."

Hail, the heaven-born Prince of Peace! Hail, the Sun of Righteousness!
Light and life to all He brings, Risen with healing in His wings.
Mild He lays His glory by, Born that man no more may die,
Born to raise the sons of earth, Born to give them second birth.
Hark, the herald angels sing, "Glory to the newborn King."

In response to the Father's gift of his Son, what gifts will you give him? The list that follows contains some items on his wish list.

• *Give the gift of self-sacrifice and commitment to God's will.* In the words of the apostle Paul, "Therefore I urge you, brethren, by the mercies of God, to present your bodies a living and holy sacrifice, acceptable to God, which is your spiritual service of worship. And do not be conformed to this world, but be transformed by the renewing of your mind, so that you may prove what the will of God is, that which is good and acceptable and perfect" (Rom. 12:1–2, NASB).

• *Return to God the gift of his faithful provision.* The apostle Paul wrote,

> "My point is this: The person who sows sparingly will also reap sparingly, and the person who sows generously will also reap generously. Each one of you should give just as he has decided in his heart, not reluctantly or under compulsion, because God loves a cheerful giver. And God is able to make all grace overflow to you so that because you have enough of everything in every way at all times, you will overflow in every good work. Just as it is written, '*He has scattered widely, he has given to the poor; his righteousness remains forever.*' Now God who provides seed for the sower and bread for food will provide and multiply your supply of seed and will cause the harvest of your righteousness to grow. You will be enriched in every way so that you may be generous on every occasion, which is producing through us thanksgiving to God, because the service of this ministry is not only providing for the needs of the saints but is also overflowing with many thanks to God. Through the evidence of this service they will glorify God because of your obedience to your confession in the gospel of Christ and the generosity of your sharing with them and with everyone. And in their prayers on your behalf they long for you because of the extraordinary grace God has shown to you. Thanks be to God for his indescribable gift!" (2 Cor. 9:6–15 NET).

• *Offer the gift of gratitude.* The writer of the Book of Hebrews exhorted his readers, "Through [Jesus] then, let us continually offer up a sacrifice of praise to God, that is, the fruit of lips that give thanks to His name. And do not neglect doing good and sharing, for with such sacrifices God is pleased" (Heb. 13:15–16, NASB).

• *Lift up praise to God for your salvation.* The apostle Peter writes, "And coming to Him as to a living stone which has been rejected by men, but is choice and precious in the sight of God, you also, as living stones, are being built up as a spiritual house for a holy priesthood, to offer up spiritual sacrifices acceptable to God through Jesus Christ" (1 Pet. 2:4–5).

When we consider the amazing presents our heavenly Father has given us, our gifts of self-sacrifice, obedience, generosity, gratitude, and praise seem small. The least we can offer in response is to worship, love, cherish, and share him with others. Will you give God the gifts on this list—presents that he desires?

Pray: In the midst of the consumerism and empty religion that plagues our culture, help me, Lord, to focus on your Son, the greatest gift. Thank you for him and for my salvation. Thank you for the hope, peace, love, and joy available to everyone who believes in him. Please help me listen to the cries of others and share the gift of your Son, the promised Messiah, throughout the year.

Memorize: "I am about to send my messenger, who will clear the way before me. Indeed, the Lord you are seeking will suddenly come to his temple, and the messenger of the covenant, whom you long for, is certainly coming," says the LORD who rules over all (Mal. 3:1).

LEADER'S GUIDE

Do you sense God leading you to facilitate a group? To lead a Coffee Cup Bible study, you do not need a seminary degree or skill at public speaking. You don't even need to have the gift of teaching. You need only a desire to see people grow through God's Word and a genuine concern for their spiritual development. Often the person best suited to the facilitator's role is not someone who likes to impart knowledge (teaching). Rather, it's someone who enjoys drawing out others and hearing them talk. Begin with prayer, asking the Lord to guide you.

GET STARTED

Pray about whom you should invite to join you. Then begin inviting participants and set a deadline for commitments. Ask yourself the best way to communicate to others the opportunity for group study—church bulletin? Web site? blog? text? e-mail? flier? poster? phone call?

If you envision a church-sponsored study with a number of small groups, aim to give participants at least several months' notice so you can schedule a room and so participants can add the event to their calendars. Work with the appropriate church staff to coordinate details of time and place.

If you plan to gather a small group of friends, decide as a group the best time and place to meet. Ideally, small groups should be limited to no more than ten members.

Take book orders, collect payment, and distribute books in advance or have each individual take care of obtaining her own. The former is recommended, however, because bulk discounts are often available; plus, people are more likely to follow through and attend if they already have a book.

Before the first meeting, determine whether to distribute studies in advance or hand them out at your kickoff. You also need to decide if members should read only the background information the first week or read the background along with completing the first week of study. If the former, plan for how you will fill the time at your first meeting, as you will have little to discuss. Perhaps you can do a service project together, such as writing to a child whom a group member sponsors. Or share your own faith story so your group can get to know you. Or read Malachi aloud as a group. (If someone prefers not to read aloud, have the group read in unison during her turn.)

Something else you'll need to decide: do you want to complete each chapter in one week or spread out your study over a longer period? If the latter, determine where to divide each week's lesson.

Obtain permission to distribute contact information among the members of your group to encourage discussion and fellowship throughout the week. Include phone, e-mail, and street-address information.

KICK IT OFF

Before your first Bible discussion time, hold a kickoff brunch or get your group together at church or a coffee shop or in a home. Pray for each person who will attend, asking that God's presence would be felt and that each woman would have a desire to learn the Word. Open with prayer.

Provide opportunities for members to get acquainted if they don't already know each other. Do this by providing introductions or asking icebreaker questions that include each participant giving her name and some background information. Ask a benign question with the potential for humor. This will help people open up to each other. For example, "What is your favorite household appliance?" (Water heater? Blender? Coffeemaker? Chocolate fountain?) One artist-led group asked this question and provided Play-Doh so each participant could make an image of her appliance for others to guess what it was.

HOLD YOUR FIRST DISCUSSION MEETING

When the group meets for the first discussion, be sure all participants meet each other if they haven't already. Distribute contact information and be sure everyone has a study book.

You will spend most of your time in discussion. If your group members hardly know each other or seem reluctant to talk, use a prepared icebreaker question to get them started. Try to come up with something that relates to the topic without requiring a spiritual answer. You may have people in your group who are completely uncomfortable talking about spiritual things, and the icebreaker is a way to help them participate in a less-threatening manner. In fact, you might want to include an icebreaker at the beginning of each discussion to get lighthearted conversation going. See the list of suggestions at the end of this chapter for possible questions for each week.

STRUCTURE YOUR WEEKLY MEETING

Begin each session with prayer and do your best to start on time, depending on the formality of the group. Set a clear ending time and respect participants' schedules.

After prayer, ask the icebreaker question, then move to discussion. Plan to allow about forty-five minutes for this time. Select the questions you'll ask by going back through the lesson for the week and choosing about seven open-ended questions. You can simply circle in your book the questions you want to ask. Be sure at least one of your choices covers what you feel is the most important point from the text for that week.

As the leader, you need to be careful not to dominate. Your job is not to instruct but to draw out. If you have a member who rarely says anything, periodically direct an easy question specifically to that person.

When you finish the final question, ask members if there was a question or issue they wanted to cover that you missed. Then ask them to share prayer requests, items for thanksgiving, and announcements. Be sure each prayer request is actually covered in prayer, and encourage the group to refrain from answering such requests with advice or related stories ("I know someone else with that kind of cancer, and she used an herbal supplement . . .").

When you're finished, be sure each person knows the next assignment as well as the meeting time and place for your next study.

Between meetings, pray for participants. It will mean a lot if you can follow up with a phone call, particularly when people have shared urgent requests. If you can make one visit to each person's home while the study is ongoing, you will likely find a huge dividend in the time invested. Just showing up and meeting people where they are goes a long way toward building community and aiding spiritual growth.

BEYOND BIBLE STUDY

Perhaps you would like to combine your time in Bible study with service. You can choose from the following ways to do so or come up with your own ideas.

Bring something to donate every week. One week, perhaps used eyeglasses. The next, it's cell phones to recycle. Then, used Bibles to go to an organization that distributes them to the needy or in countries where Bibles are not readily available. Finally, bring books to donate to the public library or your church library. Other possibilities are combining your time with a baby shower to benefit a pregnancy resource center, collecting coats for the homeless, and assembling Christmas shoe boxes for Samaritan's Purse. Involve the group in deciding what they want to do.

Combine your study with your church's missionary needs. One week, have everyone bring supplies such as energy bars, dried soup, and seeds for someone's ministry trip. Often short-term teams need items to give as gifts to translators as well as for Vacation Bible School prizes. My congregation's sister church in Mexico has asked for school supplies in September and for Spanish Bibles. Other possibilities are bringing office and bathroom supplies for your church or hosting a group garage sale and using the proceeds to grant scholarships for an activity such as the annual women's retreat.

Target a people group to learn about and pray for as part of your time together.

Adopt a missionary of the week or month to correspond with, pray for, and learn about each time you meet.

Choose a group within your community to serve. If a nursing home, visit it together one week and take some large-print Bibles or other books. Or volunteer to pick up trash in an area where your city has a need. Or take a fruit basket to your local firefighters.

Work together as a group on a craft to donate, such as sewing blankets for a women's shelter. Local homeless shelters often have ongoing demand for pillowcases—which are easy to make. Or learn to knit and donate scarves to the homeless to help them through long winters.

By linking time in God's Word with time serving others, you will help group members move from compartmentalizing to integrating their discipleship time and the stewardship of their resources.

Lists of and links to additional helps for your Bible discussion time are available at aspire2.com in the Coffee Cup Bible Studies section of the site. If your group generates ideas they want to share with others, send them through the contact page on the site. We'd love to know what worked for you.

Perhaps you have some artists or musicians in your group who need more right-brained interaction. Songs, jewelry, paintings, photos, collages, poetry, prayers, psalms—the options for creative interaction in response to the truths learned in Malachi are endless. Someone might want to come up with a music playlist that will help you learn verses from Malachi set to music.

Finally, if you are meeting at a coffee shop or restaurant, learn the name of your barista or server and the person cleaning your table. You may be the only people they meet all day who seem to care.

DISCUSSION STARTERS

Remember that icebreaker questions are simply to get discussion started. When you open with an easy question, everyone should be able to answer. No one should feel intimidated. If you wish, craft questions that better fit your own group. You could also craft your own questions that relate to the theme of each week of Advent: hope, peace, love, and joy.

Week 1. The people in Malachi's day were guilty of bringing God their unwanted leftovers. So begin your group time by having each person describe her or her family's unfortunate experience with leftovers—perhaps a flopped attempt to make a side dish from leftover turkey or an attempt at regifting that went badly. The goal here is not to get everyone complaining but to keep the mood light while also providing a transition to the lesson topic.

Advent Week 1: For an Advent emphasis on hope, talk about the difference between "I hope so" hope and "I know so" hope. Come prepared to share something for which you hoped for a long time that finally happened—perhaps the birth of a child, the opportunity to visit a special destination, or seeing the reconciliation of warring parties. Sing: "O Come, O Come, Emmanuel."

Week 2. Part of the discussion during week two focuses on how spiritual leaders should act and how a righteous person views marriage. Ask each member to describe someone whose spiritual leadership or marriage they admire and why.

Advent Week 2: For an Advent emphasis on peace, read the article below and come ready to discuss how you can have a more peace-filled celebration of the arrival of the Prince of Peace.

TEN STEPS TO A SANER CHRISTMAS SEASON

It doesn't have to happen again—the insane pace, the big-dollar debt, and the no-time-for-the-main-thing rush in the hustle and bustle. With a little forethought, about thirty minutes today, we can get it right over the time between now and Christmas. Our celebration of the Lord's coming can reflect our honor for him rather than neglect. The theme for week two of Advent is peace. Jesus is the Prince of Peace! And that peace is available to the entire world, but also in our individual lives. Start with prayer and consider these suggestions for a more peace-filled, Christ-centered holiday season.

• *Decide when to spend time in study and prayer.* Schedule it. Plan for it.

• *Be intentional about giving.* First, the charitable donations. Over the next month worthy causes will bombard you with requests. Rather than grumbling about it, give thanks that so many good organizations exist. Pray about how much and to whom you can give. Next, consider gift giving for the people on your Christmas list. Think about ways to give of yourself. For example, a family member might appreciate receiving a favorite aunt's recipe in a basket with all the ingredients.

Also give to benefit others. Purchase fair-trade jewelry. Or donate a goat to an impoverished family and give it in honor of someone who doesn't need another pink lamp. Give books that inspire, music that lifts the heart, and even cooking, knitting, or art classes instead of expensive junk. If you have no money, consider how to offer the gift of your time—redeemable in January. Or perhaps you can sell some used books or that old bike in the garage? Take ten minutes now to plan ahead. One friend wrote me to say, "We are skipping Christmas gifts this year and saving our money to take a family trip. I feel so free from all the glitzy marketing. It's liberating."

• *Write to encourage.* If you sponsor a child, write him or her a letter and tuck inside a bookmark or Christmas stickers. Send a card to a member of the military who's far from home this year: If you teach a Sunday school class or lead a Girl Scout troop, help them compose a group letter. As for cards or letters to your own friends, determine whether you want to send those this year. If so, think about how to keep them simple, warm, humble, and Christ-honoring.

• *Embrace a free tradition.* Why not add a simple practice that deepens the season's meaning? You could place your crèche in a central location but leave the cradle empty until Christmas morning, when you make a grand celebration of the baby's arrival. Or read one chapter of Dickens's *A Christmas Carol* at the dinner table nightly. (The story is often available as a free Kindle download, but your public library probably has a copy or two as well.) Or schedule a family night of popcorn with root beer floats, and watch *A Charlie Brown Christmas.*

• *Fill your life with worship sounds.* Christmas brings a great opportunity to publicly and privately listen to inspiring music. Pull out or download Handel's *Messiah*—which includes some songs based on Malachi's message. Put some CDs in the car to add joy to your drive time.

• *Think about who needs you to listen.* My Christian journalist friends tell me that "listening is the new apologetic." In the craziness of the season, some deeply hurting people get overlooked. Think about who would appreciate a phone call or an invitation to an event you're already attending, such as your church's musical. To whom can you bring peace in this season?

• *Remember the hurting.* Christmas can bring additional agony to those who have suffered loss. Give Christ the gift of your compassion expressed to someone in pain.

• *Lower your expectations and prune your perfectionism.* Make your holiday party a dessert event and forget cooking a full dinner. Promise yourself you'll focus on spending time with loved ones, not on sparkling bathrooms or presents.

- *Declutter and donate.* Take a load out of your purse and encourage that Salvation Army bell ringer with lots of coins clinking. Send your stack of extra Bibles to an organization that gives them new owners. Collect your extra bedding, pillowcases, and coats, and set them aside to deliver to a women's shelter—in January.
- *Decide what you want for Christmas.* When people ask, "What can I get you?" provide them with suggestions of items you truly want or give them the name of your favorite charity. If you think ahead, you're more likely to receive what you can truly use instead of one more fruitcake.
- *Cut back.* Really do it. Defy commercialization and give of yourself. Start with scheduling downtime in the same way you would schedule cooking and shopping time—go ahead and mark off those days today. (Maybe this would be a good time to find out the dates of church and office parties and the kids' concerts and musicals (so the I-need-a-costume demand doesn't catch you by surprise). De-stress with prayer, stretching exercises, hot peppermint tea, and sticking to your boundaries.
- *Examine your attitude.* The people in Malachi's day had the attitude that God was obliged to accept whatever they gave him. Search your heart for where you might have a similar attitude and pray for an attitude that says, "All I have is rightfully yours. I offer back to you a fraction of all that belongs to you."

For Christmas, Jesus wants a present too—all of you. Ask him to help you bring an excellent offering this year.

Week 3. In the narrative portion of week three's study, we discuss gifts and giving. Have each person describe a time when she thoroughly enjoyed giving a gift. What was the gift and who was it for? Why was it a joy to give?

Advent Week 3: For an Advent emphasis on love, include a discussion about a time when love motivated you to give something special. Describe the relationship you had/have with the person to whom you gave a special gift. Explain why you wanted to give. Sing "Oh, the Deep, Deep Love of Jesus" or "How Deep the Father's Love for Us."

Week 4. During the four hundred silent years, God was preparing the nation of Israel for the first advent of his son. Share a time when you prepared something special, whether it was a meal, a gift, or the visit of a guest.

Advent Week 4: For an Advent emphasis on joy, describe a situation that brought you joy and/or search for information on C. S. Lewis's wonderful writings on joy and *Sehnsucht,* and talk about them. If you prefer to focus on a theme of preparation that goes with the 400 Silent Years, ask, "How do your families prepare for Christmas? What are some of your favorite before-Christmas traditions?" Sing "Joy to the World."

About the NET BIBLE®

The NET BIBLE® is an exciting new translation of the Bible with 60,932 translators' notes! These translators' notes make the original Greek, Hebrew and Aramaic texts of the Bible far more accessible and unlocks the riches of the Bible's truth from entirely new perspectives.

The NET BIBLE® is the first modern Bible to be completely free for anyone, anywhere in the world to download as part of a powerful new "Ministry First" approach being pioneered at bible.org.

Download the entire NET Bible and 60,932 notes for free at www.bible.org

About the bible.org ministry

Before there was eBay® . . . before there was Amazon.com® . . . there was bible.org! Bible.org is a non-profit (501c3) Christian ministry headquartered in Dallas, Texas. In the last decade bible.org has grown to serve millions of individuals around the world and provides thousands of trustworthy resources for Bible study (2 Tim 2:2).

Go to www.bible.org for thousands of trustworthy resources including:

- The NET BIBLE®
- Discipleship Materials
- The Theology Program
- More than 10,000 Sermon Illustrations
- ABC's of Christian Growth
- Bible Dictionaries and Commentaries

Made in United States
Orlando, FL
24 June 2022